Fields of force

V 1862- Bjerknes

PUBLICATION NUMBER ONE

OF THE

ERNEST KEMPTON ADAMS FUND FOR PHYSICAL RESEARCH

Established December 17, 1904

FIELDS OF FORCE

A COURSE OF LECTURES IN MATHEMATICAL PHYSICS

DELIVERED DECEMBER 1 TO 23, 1905

BY

VILHELM FRIMAN KOREN BJERKNES

PROFESSOR OF MECHANICS AND MATHEMATICAL PHYSICS IN THE UNIVERSITY OF STOCKHOLM
LECTURER IN MATHEMATICAL PHYSICS IN COLUMBIA UNIVERSITY, 1905-6

New York
THE COLUMBIA UNIVERSITY PRESS
THE MACMILLAN COMPANY, Agents
LONDON: MACMILLAN CO., Ltd.
1906

On the seventeenth day of December nineteen hundred and four, Edward Dean Adams, of New York, established in Columbia University "The Ernest Kempton Adams Fund for Physical Research" as a memorial to his son, Ernest Kempton Adams, who received the degrees of Electrical Engineering in 1897 and Master of Arts in 1898, and who devoted his life to scientific research. The income of this fund is, by the terms of the deed of gift, to be devoted to the maintenance of a research fellowship and to the publication and distribution of the results of scientific research on the part of the fellow. A generous interpretation of the terms of the deed on the part of Mr. Adams and of the Trustees of the University has made it possible to print and distribute the following lectures as a publication of the Ernest Kempton Adams Fund:

FIELDS OF FORCE.

I.

ELEMENTARY INVESTIGATION OF THE GEO-METRIC PROPERTIES OF HYDRO-DYNAMIC FIELDS.

INTRODUCTORY.

The idea of electric and magnetic fields of force was intro-duced by FARADAY to avoid the mysterious idea of an action at a distance. After the victory which MAXWELL'S theory gained through the experiments of HERTZ, the idea of these fields took its place among the most fruitful of theoretical physics.

And yet if we ask, what *is* an electric or a magnetic field of force? no one will be able to give a satisfactory answer. We have theories relating to these fields, but we have no idea whatever of what they *are* intrinsically, nor even the slightest idea of the path to follow in order to discover their true nature. Above all other problems which are related to fields of force, and which occupy investigators daily, we have therefore *the* problem of fields of force, viz., the problem of their true nature.

My lectures will not give the solution of this problem, but I should be happy if they should contribute to a broadening of our view of it.

What I wish to insist upon especially, is this. Besides elec-tric and magnetic fields there exist other fields which have strik-ingly analogous properties, and which have, therefore, exactly the same claim to be called fields of force. The investigation of these other fields side by side with the electric and magnetic fields will be advantageous, I think, in broadening our view of the problem, especially as the true nature of these other fields of force is per-

1   1

fectly plain and intelligible, as intelligible, at least, as anything
can be in the limited state of our power of understanding

These other fields of force exist in material media which are
in suitable states of motion   They are perfectly intelligible in
this sense, that their properties can be deduced from the principles
of dynamics   For the special case when the material medium is a
perfect fluid, the properties of these fields have been extensively
explored, and therefore our main subject will be the investigation
of the properties of hydrodynamic fields of force and their comparison with electric or magnetic fields

The results which I shall bring before you were discovered
originally by my late father, Professor C A BJERKNES, of Christiania   But I will bring into application here new methods, which
allow us to find the results with much greater generality, and at the
same time with greater facility *

My lectures will be divided into two parts   The first two lectures will be devoted to the development of the properties of hydrodynamic fields by elementary reasoning and experiment, the
following lectures will give the analytical investigation of the same
subject, based upon EULER's equations of motion for a perfect
fluid and MAXWELL's equations for the electromagnetic field

1   *Field-vectors* —The electric field may be described in the
simplest case by either of two vectors, the electric *flux* (or displacement), or the electric *field intensity* (or force)   In the same
way the magnetic field may be described by the magnetic *flux* (or
induction), or the magnetic *field intensity* (or force)   The flux and
the field intensity will differ from each other only by a constant
factor, the electric or the magnetic *inductivity* of the medium which
supports the field, the flux being always the product of the field
intensity into the inductivity

* For the historical development of C A Bjerknes' ideas compare *v Bjerknes
C A Bjerknes, Gedachtnissrede gehalten in der Gesellschaft der Wissenschaften zu
Christiania am April, 1903*   German translation, Leipzig, 1903   For the development of the theory according to C A Bjerknes' methods, and for more
complete description of instruments and experiments, see *v Bjerknes, Vorlesungen
uber hydrodynamische Fernkräfte nach C A Bjerknes' Theorie*   Vols I and II
Leipzig, 1900–02

On the other hand, the field of motion in any moving liquid may also be described by either of two vectors, which are related to each other in the same way as the flux and the field intensity of electric or magnetic fields. The first of these vectors is the *velocity*, and the other the *product of the velocity into the density* As to its dynamical significance, this vector is the momentum per unit volume or the *specific momentum* in the moving fluid

In hydrodynamics we thus meet with two vectors which are connected in a similar way as the flux and the field intensity in the electric or magnetic field This parallelism at once invites a comparison There is only the question as to how the different vectors should be paired, and this can be answered only by a closer analysis of their properties This brings us to the question of our knowledge of the fields

2 *Geometric and Dynamic Properties of the Fields* — The extent of our knowledge of the different kinds of fields differs greatly All the properties of the hydrodynamic fields follow directly from the most trustworthy laws of nature, that is from the principle of the conservation of the mass, and from the principles of dynamics With reference to electric or magnetic fields, on the contrary, we have only formal theories First, we have an extensively developed *geometric theory of the distribution in space of the vectors* which describe the field And then, in a more or less superficial connection to this geometric theory, we have a very much less developed theory of the *dynamic properties of the fields*

Taking the facts as they lie before us, we shall be obliged, therefore, to give to our theory a dualistic form, comparing separately the geometric and the dynamic properties of the two kinds of fields It may be reserved for the future to penetrate to the central point, where the geometry and the dynamics of the question are perfectly united, and thus make the comparison of the two kinds of fields perfectly easy

In this lecture we will consider the geometric properties of the fields

3 *Properties of the Field Vectors at a Surface of Separation* —
A characteristic geometrical property of the vectors at a surface of
separation of two media shows at once how the fluxes and field
intensities should be paired with the hydrodynamic vectors   As
is well known, at a surface of separation the normal component
of the flux is always continuous, while the normal component of
the field intensity is necessarily discontinuous, if the inductivity
suddenly changes at the surface   On the other hand, at any surface of separation in a moving liquid the normal component of the
velocity is continuous, corresponding to the normal component of
the flux   Otherwise we should have at the surface either creation
or annihilation of matter, or a break in the continuity, both of
which we consider excluded   From the continuity of the normal
component of the velocity follows the discontinuity of the specific
momentum for the case where the density of the fluid suddenly
changes at the surface   This vector, therefore, has a discontinuity
similar to that of the field intensity, and it follows at once that the
correspondence of the vectors is possible if the velocity correspond
to the flux and the specific momentum to the field intensity   Further, as the flux is the product of the field intensity into the inductivity, it also follows that not the density, but the reciprocal of the
density, or the specific volume, corresponds to the inductivity

Just as the density gives the measure of the inert resistance of
the matter to the motion, the specific volume gives the measure of
the readiness of the matter to take motion   The specific volume
may therefore also be termed the *mobility* of the fluid   We thus
get the correspondence

velocity	flux,
specific momentum	field intensity,
mobility	inductivity

We have now to examine more closely the content of this
correspondence

4 *Charged Particle — Expanding or Contracting Particle* —
Let us start with the simplest object met with in the first investi-

gations of electricity, namely, with an electrically charged particle
In the field belonging to this particle the vectors are directed
radially outwards if the particle has a positive, and radially inwards if it has a negative charge, and their intensity decreases as
the inverse square of the distance

It is seen at once that an expanding particle which is contained
in an incompressible fluid, such as water, will produce a field of
exactly the same geometrical nature as the field belonging to the
positively charged particle It will produce a radial current
directed outwards, in which, as a consequence of the incompressi-
bility, the velocity, and therefore the specific momentum will decrease as the inverse square of the distance In like manner a contracting particle will be surrounded by a current directed radially
inwards, and will thus correspond to a negatively charged particle
(see Fig 4, *a* and *b*, below)

This comparison of a radial electric and a radial hydrodynamic
field has one difficulty, however The idea of an always expanding, or of an always contracting particle, is impossible Therefore
to make the comparison possible, not only for a moment, but for
any length of time, we are obliged to consider a motion of periodic expansions and contractions, or a *pulsating* motion In this
case there will be no absolute difference between a positive and a
negative pulsating body But two pulsating bodies may be in
exactly the same *mutual* relation to each other as an expanding
and a contracting body For if they are pulsating in opposite phase, the one will always be expanding while the other is
contracting, and vice versa We can then distinguish these two
pulsating bodies from each other by opposite signs, just as we
do two oppositely charged particles, and we can represent the
mean state of motion in the surrounding radial field by a vector
directed outwards from the pulsating particle which we call, by
convention, positive, and inwards to the pulsating particle which
we call negative

5 *Complex Fields* — If we consider two charged particles
whose dimensions are sufficiently small in comparison to the dis-

tance between them, a field is produced which is the simple result of the superposition of the two radial fields   The lines of force of the complex fields may be found by the well-known constructions of superposition   The results are the well known curves running from one charged particle to the other for the case of opposite charges, and the diverging curves with a neutral point between the two charged particles for the case of charges of the same sign (see Figs 5 and 6 below)

In exactly the same way, if we consider two particles which have a motion of expansion or contraction and which are sufficiently small in comparison to the distance between them, the radial currents produced by each will simply be superposed, and the current lines, by which the complex field may be represented, can be found by exactly the same construction as in the case of the corresponding electric fields   And this result may be transferred at once to the case of vibratory motion, particles pulsating in the same phase, expanding simultaneously and contracting simultaneously, will give a field corresponding geometrically to that produced by particles carrying charges of the same sign, and oppositely pulsating particles will produce a field corresponding geometrically to that produced by particles which carry opposite charges

Just as we combine the fields of two charged particles, we can combine the fields of any number of charged particles, and to a field of any complexity obtained in this way we can construct a corresponding hydrodynamic field, obtained by the combination of the fields of the corresponding system of expanding and contracting particles, or of pulsating particles for the case of vibratory motion An extensive geometric analogy between hydrodynamic and electrostatic fields is thus found

6 *Intrinsically Polarized Bodies   Oscillating Bodies* — What we have said of electrified particles and the electric fields produced by them may be repeated for magnetic poles and the corresponding magnetic fields   But now the reservation must be made, that magnetic poles are in reality mere fictions   For a distribution of

magnetic poles we can, however, substitute a state of intrinsic polarization, which may be considered as the real origin of the magnetic field Such states of intrinsic polarization are also met with in electricity. Thus the pyro-electric crystal seems to give a perfect electric analogy to the permanent magnet

Let us now for the system of magnetic poles by which a magnet can be represented symbolically, substitute the corresponding system of expanding and contracting particles. In the region of the fluid which corresponds to the magnet the total sum of expansions and contractions will be zero But the field produced in the exterior space by these expansions and contractions may also be produced by quite another interior motion, involving no expansion or contraction at all For consider a closed surface consisting of fluid particles, and surrounding the region of the fluid which corresponds to the magnet This material surface has a certain motion , it will advance on that side where the expanding particles are situated, and recede on that side where the contracting particles are situated The result is a motion of the surface as a whole, directed from the regions of contraction towards the regions of expansion And, as the sum of the expansions and the contractions is zero, the volume within the surface will remain unchanged during this motion

Now the motion produced outside the surface will be entirely independent of what goes on within it, provided only that the motion of the surface itself remains unchanged We can therefore do away with the expansions and contractions and suppose the volume within the surface filled with an incompressible fluid, subject to the action of forces which give these fluid masses a motion consistent with the required motion of the surface

We have thus arrived at the following result a motion of incompressible fluid masses produced by suitable forces, can be found which will set up an exterior field similar to that set up by a system of expanding and contracting particles, provided that the sum of the expansions and contractions is zero And this equivalence corresponds exactly to the equivalence between the representation of a magnet by a distribution of poles, and by a state of intrinsic polarization The hydrodynamic model of a body in a state of intrinsic polarization is, therefore, a body consisting of incompressible fluid masses, moved through the surrounding fluid by suitable exterior forces (see Fig 8 below)

We have considered here, for simplicity, only the instantaneous state of motion In the case of periodic motion we get an equivalence between a system of oppositely pulsating particles and a fluid body which takes forced oscillations under the influence of suitable exterior forces

7 *Fields in Heterogeneous Media* — The results already developed depend, essentially upon the supposition that the fluid surrounding the moving bodies is homogeneous and incompressible The case when it is heterogeneous must be examined separately That the heterogeneity has an influence upon the geometric configuration of the field, is obvious For only when the fluid is perfectly homogeneous will there exist that perfect symmetry in the space surrounding an expanding particle which entitles us to conclude that a perfectly symmetrical radial current will arise But if on one side of the expanding particle there exists a region where the fluid has a different density, the symmetry is lost, and it is to be expected that the configuration of the field will be influenced by this fact On the other hand, as is well known, any heterogeneity of the dielectric has a marked influence upon the geometric configuration of the electric field, giving rise to the phenomena of electrification by influence

Now, will the influence of the heterogeneity in the two cases be of similar nature? To examine this question we shall have to develop a very simple principle relating to the dynamics of fluids, our considerations above having been based only on the principle of the conservation of mass

8 *Principle of Kinetic Buoyancy* — Consider a cylinder, with axis vertical containing a body and, apart from the body, completely filled with water The condition of equilibrium will depend upon the buoyancy, according to the Archimedian principle If the body

has exactly the density of the water, the buoyancy will balance the weight of the body, and it will remain in equilibrium in any position If it be lighter, its buoyancy will be greater than its weight, and it will tend to move upwards. If it be heavier, its buoyancy will be less than its weight, and it will tend to move downwards Thus, if we have three cylinders, each containing one of three such bodies, the light body will rise to the top, the heavy body will sink to the bottom, and the body of the same density as the water will remain in any position

This static buoyancy depends upon the action of gravity But there exists a corresponding dynamic buoyancy, which is easily observed as follows To do away with the influence of gravity, lay the cylinders with their axes horizontal, and let the bodies be in the middle of the cylinders. Then give each cylinder a blow, so that they move suddenly five or ten centimeters in the direction of their axes The following results will then be observed

1 The body which is lighter than the water has moved towards the front end of its cylinder, and thus has had a motion through the water in the direction of the motion of the water

2. The body which has the same density as the water has moved exactly the same distance as the water, and thus retained its position relative to the water

3 The body which is heavier than the water has moved a shorter distance than its cylinder, and thus has had a motion through the water against the direction of motion of the water

If we give the cylinders a series of blows, the light body will advance through the water until it stops against the front end The body of the same density as the water will retain its place, and the heavy body will move backwards relatively to the cylinder, until it stops against the end The effect is strikingly analogous to the effect of statical buoyancy for the case of the cylinders with vertical axes, and this analogy exists even in the quantitative laws of the phenomenon

These quantitative laws are complicated in case the bodies are

2

free to move through the water, but exceedingly simple when they
are held in an invariable position relative to the water by the
application of suitable exterior forces

This exterior force is nil in the case when the body has the
same density as the water The body then follows the motion of
the surrounding water masses, subject only to the force resulting
from the pressure exerted by them The motion of the body is
subject to the fundamental law of dynamics,

$$\text{force} = \text{mass} \times \text{acceleration}$$

As the body has both the acceleration and the density of the
surrounding water masses, the force is equal to the product of the
acceleration into the mass of the water displaced by the body
And this law evidently will be true even for the heavy or the
light body, provided only that they are held by suitable forces at
rest relatively to the moving water For, the state of motion outside the body is then unchanged, and the pressure exerted by the
water against any surface does not at all depend upon the conditions within the surface Thus we find this general result, which
is perfectly analogous to the Archimedian law

*Any body which participates in the translatory motion of a fluid
mass is subject to a kinetic buoyancy equal to the product of the
acceleration of the translatory motion multiplied by the mass of water
displaced by the body*

This law obviously gives also the value of the exterior force
which must be applied in order to make the body follow exactly
the motion of the fluid, just as the Archimedian law gives the
force which is necessary to prevent a body from rising or sinking
This force is nil, if the body has the same density as the water, it
is directed against the direction of the acceleration, if the body is
lighter, and in the direction of the acceleration, if the body is
heavier And, if no such force act, we get the result, illustrated
by the experiment, that the light body moves faster than the
water and the heavy body slower, and thus, relatively, against the
water

9 *Influence of Heterogeneities in the Electric or Magnetic and in the Analogous Hydrodynamic Field* — From the principle of kinetic buoyancy we thus find the obvious law, that, in a heterogeneous fluid, masses of greater mobility take greater velocities The mobility therefore influences the distribution of velocity, just as the inductivity influences the distribution of the flux in the electric, or magnetic field For at places of greater inductivity we have greater electric, or magnetic flux

To consider a simple example, let us place in a bottle filled with water a light sphere, a hollow celluloid ball, for instance, attached below with a fine string And in another bottle let us suspend in a similar manner a lead ball If we shake the bottles, the celluloid ball will take very lively oscillations, much greater than those of the water, while the lead ball will remain almost at rest With respect to their induced oscillations, they behave, then, exactly as magnetic or diamagnetic bodies behave with respect to the induced magnetization when they are brought into a magnetic field, the light body takes greater oscillations than the water, just as the magnetic body takes greater magnetization than the surrounding medium The heavy body, on the other hand, takes smaller oscillations than the water, just as the diamagnetic body takes smaller magnetization than the surrounding medium And thus relatively, the heavy body has oscillations opposite to those of the water, just as the diamagnetic has a relative polarity opposite to that of the surrounding medium

10 *Refraction of the Lines of Flow* — The influence which the greater velocity of the masses of greater mobility has upon the course of the tubes of flow is obvious. At places of greater velocity the tubes of flow narrow, and at places of smaller velocity widen They will thus be narrow at places of great, and wide at places of small *mobility*, just as the tubes of flux in the electric or magnetic field are narrow at places of great, and wide at places of small *inductivity* If we limit ourselves to the consideration of the most practical case, when the values of the mobility or of the inductivity change abruptly at certain surfaces, we can easily prove

that the influence of the heterogeneity in the two kinds of fields corresponds not only qualitativity but quantitatively.

We suppose that the bodies which have other density than the surrounding fluid are themselves fluid. It is only in experiments that, for practical reasons, we must always use rigid bodies. At the surface of separation between the surrounding fluid and the fluid body the pressure must have the same value on both sides of the surface. This is an immediate consequence of the principle of equal action and reaction. From the equality of the pressure on both sides of the surface it follows, that the rate of decrease of the pressure in direction tangential to the surface is also equal at adjacent points on each side of the surface. But this rate of decrease is the gradient, or the force per unit volume, in the moving fluid. And, as the acceleration produced by the force per unit volume is inversely proportional to the density, we find that the tangential acceleration on the two sides of the surface of separation will be inversely proportional to the density. Or, what is the same thing, *the product of the tangential acceleration into the density will have the same value on both sides of the surface.*

From this result there can not at once be drawn a general conclusion on the relation of the tangential components of the velocity, or of the specific momentum. For two adjacent particles, which are accelerated according to this law, will at the next moment no longer be adjacent. If, however, the motion be periodic, so that every particle has an invariable mean position, then adjacent particles will remain adjacent particles, and from the equality of the tangential components of the products of the accelerations into the densities at once follows the equality of the tangential components of the products of the velocities into the densities. Thus,

In the case of vibratory motion the specific momentum has continuous tangential components at the surface of separation of two media of different mobility.

The law for the specific momentum is thus exactly the same as for the electric or magnetic field intensities, which have continuous tangential components at the surface of separation of two media of different inductivity   As we have already found (3), the law for the velocity is the same as for the electric or the magnetic flux   We see then, that the conditions fulfilled at a surface of separation by the hydrodynamic vectors on the one hand, and by the electric or magnetic vectors on the other, are identically the same   The lines of flow and the lines of flux will show exactly the same peculiarity in passing a surface of separation And, as is shown in all treatises on electricity, this peculiarity consists in a refraction of the lines so that the tangents of the angles of incidence and refraction are in the same ratio as the inductivities on the two sides of the surface   In the hydrodynamic case these tangents will be in the same ratio as the mobilities on the two sides of the surface   This refraction gives to the tubes of flow or of flux the sudden change of section which corresponds to the increase or decrease of the velocity or of the flux in passing from one medium into the other

This refraction of the hydrodynamic lines of flow according to the same law as that of the refraction of the electric or magnetic lines of force is a phenomenon met with daily in the motion of superimposed liquids of different specific weights   If I suddenly move a glass partly filled with mercury and partly with water, the mercury rises along the rear wall of the glass, while the water sinks in front. During the first instant of the motion, before we get the oscillations due to gravity, the law of the refraction of the tubes of flow is fulfilled at the surface of separation   Whatever be the course of the tubes of flow at a distance from the surface, at the surface they will be refracted so that the tangents of the angles of incidence and of refraction are in the ratio of the mobilities of the mercury and of the water, or in the inverse ratio of their densities, 1 . 13

We get the same law of refraction at the surface of separation of water and air, the tangents of the angles being then in the ratio, 1 · 700   The accident of daily occurrence, in which a glass of water flows over as the result of sudden motion, is thus the consequence of a law strictly analogous to that of the refraction of the electric or magnetic lines of force

11. *Experimental Verifications.* — We have been able from kinematic and dynamic principles of the simplest nature to show the existence of an extended analogy in the geometric properties of the electric or magnetic, and hydrodynamic fields. The dynamic principles which form the basis of this analogy we have illustrated by experiments of the simplest possible nature. But even though we have perfect faith in the truth of the results, it is desirable to see direct verifications of them. Some experiments have been made towards finding verifications, but not as many, however, as might have been desirable.

These experiments were made with water motions of vibratory nature, produced by pulsating or oscillating bodies, using instruments constructed mainly for the investigation of the dynamic properties of the field, which will be the subject of the next lecture. Such pulsations and oscillations can easily be produced by a pneumatic arrangement involving a generator which produces an alternating current of air.

12. *The Generator.* — A generator of this kind consists of two small air pumps of the simplest possible construction, without valves. To avoid metal work we can simply use drums, covered with rubber membranes, which are alternately pressed in and drawn out. These pumps should be arranged so that they can work in either the same or in opposite phase, and so that the amplitudes of the strokes of each pump can be varied independently of the other. For convenience, it should be possible to reverse the phase and vary the amplitudes without interrupting the motion of the generator.

In Fig. 1 is shown a generator, arranged to fulfill these conditions. In a wooden base are fixed two vertical steel or brass springs, *s*, which are joined by the horizontal connecting-rod, *b*. The upper ends of these springs are connected by the piston-rods, *a*, to the pistons of the air-pumps, which are supported on a wooden frame in such a way that each is free to turn about a horizontal axis, *c*, passing through the top of the corresponding spring perpendicular to the piston-rod. Thus either pump can be revolved through 180°, or through a smaller angle, without stopping the pumps. The amplitude of the strokes in any position is proportional to the cosine of this angle, since the component of the motion of the top of the spring along the axis of the cylinder is proportional to this cosine. At 90° the amplitude is 0, and the phase changes, so that by a simple rotation we are able to reverse the phase, or vary the amplitude of either, or both pumps.

The generator may be driven by a motor of suitable nature, attached to the frame. As shown in the figure, we may use a fly-wheel, d, carrying a crank which drives the springs, using an

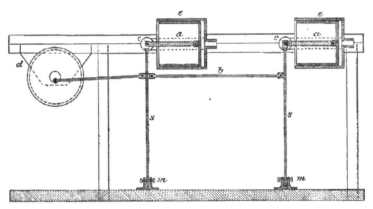

FIG. 1.

electric motor, or any other suitable source, for motive power. The use of the crank has the advantage that the amplitudes of the oscillations of the springs are invariable and independent of the resistance to the motion. It should be noted here, that, with the crank, the springs may be used simply as rigid levers, by loosening the screws, m, which hold them in the base. The springs are then free to turn about a pivot just below the screws.

A hydraulic motor might also be used to drive the generator. Two coaxial brass cylinders, open at the same end, are so arranged that the inner projects slightly beyond the outer. A rubber membrane is stretched over the open ends of the two tubes, so that water admitted to the outer cylinder cannot pass into the inner cylinder without pressing out the membrane.　Under suitable circumstances, this produces a vibration of the membrane,

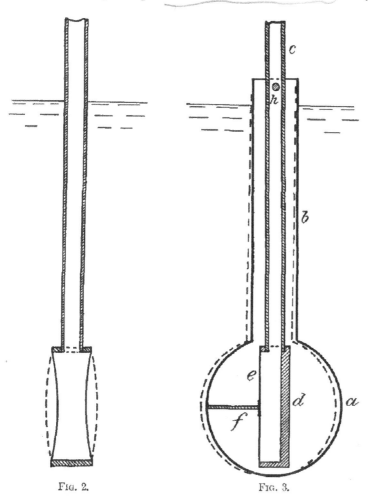

FIG. 2.　　　　　　　　FIG. 3.

which can be communicated to the pumps by the connecting-rods. The period will depend upon the tension of the membrane, the stiffness of the springs, and the length and section of the discharge-pipe An electromagnetic vibrator is often convenient for driving the generator

13 *Pulsator Oscillator* — For a pulsating body we may use an india-rubber balloon attached to one end of a metal tube, the other end of which is connected by a rubber tube with one of the pumps of the generator As the balloon often takes irregular forms and motions, it is usually more convenient to let the tube end in a drum, which is covered on each side with a rubber membrane A diagram is given in Fig 2

A convenient form of oscillator is shown in Fig 3 The oscillating body is a hollow celluloid sphere, *a*, made in two halves, and attached to a tube of the same material, *b*, which reaches above the surface of the water A metal tube, *c*, connected with one pump of the generator, supports the sphere by pivots at *h*, and terminates in a heavy drum, *d*, in the center of the sphere The rubber membrane, *e*, is connected with one side of the sphere by a rod, *f*, so that the alternating air current produces oscillations in the sphere and in the drum The sphere is made as light as possible and the drum heavy, so that, while the former takes large oscillations, the latter will take very small oscillations because of its greater mass For convenience in recognizing the axis of oscillation the two halves of the sphere may be painted in different colors, so that, at any moment, the advancing hemisphere is one color and the receding hemisphere another Thus, two oscillators connected with pumps in the same phase have hemispheres of the same color advancing simultaneously

14 *Instrument for the Registering of Water Oscillations* — When a pulsating or an oscillating body, like one of those just described, is placed in the water, the motion produced by it cannot be seen, as an obvious consequence of the transparency of the water This motion can, however, be observed indirectly in several ways For example, we can suspend small particles in the water and observe their motions, and we might even succeed in getting photographs of the paths of oscillation of the suspended

3

particles. This method has, however, never been used, and may involve difficulties because of the small amplitudes of the oscillations.

A more mechanical method, depending upon the principle of kinetic buoyancy, is preferable. A body which is situated in the oscillating masses of fluid will be subject to a periodic kinetic buoyancy which tries to set up in it oscillations of the same direction as those of the water. The amplitudes of the oscillations produced will, however, generally be minute, but they may be increased by resonance. The body is fixed upon an elastic wire, and the period of the generator varied until it accords with the period of the free vibrations of the body. The amplitude of the oscillations of the body is then greatly increased.

The body is made to carry a hair pencil, which reaches above the surface of the water. One or two millimeters above the point of the brush is placed a horizontal glass plate, resting upon springs. When the body has acquired large oscillations, the glass plate may be pressed down and the brush marks an ink line upon it. The registering device is then moved to another place in the fluid, and the direction of the water oscillations at this place recorded on the glass plate, and so on. In this way complete diagrams of the lines of oscillation in the fluid are obtained.

15. *Diagrams of Hydrodynamic and Corresponding Magnetic Fields.*—Figs. 4–8, *a*, give diagrams of hydrodynamic fields obtained in this way, while Figs. 4–8, *b*, give the diagrams of the corresponding magnetic fields, obtained in the well known way with iron filings.

Fig. 4, *a*, gives the radial lines of oscillation obtained in the space around a pulsating body, while Fig. 4, *b*, gives the corresponding magnetic lines of force issuing from one pole of a long bar magnet.

Fig. 5, *a*, gives the lines of oscillation produced in the fluid by two bodies pulsating in the same phase. They represent the meeting of two radial currents issuing from two centers. Fig. 5, *b*, gives the perfectly analogous representation of the magnetic lines of force issuing from two magnetic poles of the same sign.

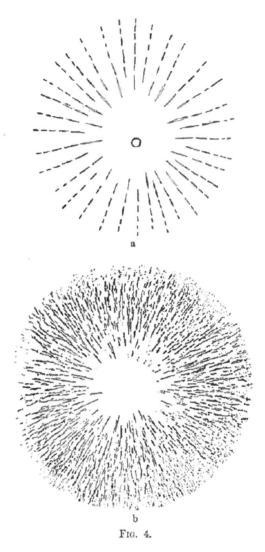

FIG. 4.

Fig. 6, *a*, gives the lines of oscillation produced in the fluid by two bodies pulsating in opposite phase.   The diagram gives the representation of a current which diverges from one pulsating body and converges toward the other. Fig. 6, *b*, gives the perfectly analogous representation of the magnetic lines of force produced by two magnetic poles of opposite sign.

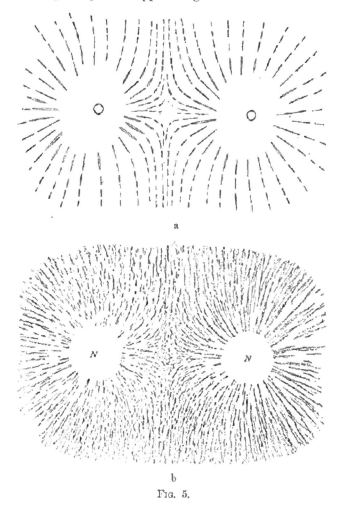

a

b

Fig. 5.

Fig. 7, *a*, gives the more complicated representation of the line of oscillation produced in the water by a combination of three pulsating bodies, two pulsating in the same phase, and one in the opposite, and Fig. 7, *b*, gives the perfectly analogous representation of the magnetic lines of force produced by three magnetic poles, of which two have the same sign, and one the opposite.

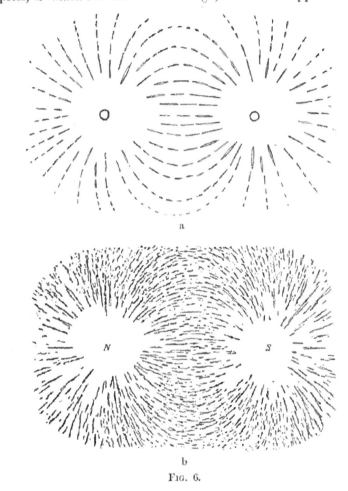

a

b

FIG. 6.

Finally, Fig. 8, *a*, gives the lines of oscillation produced in the fluid by an oscillating body, and Fig. 8, *b*, the corresponding lines of magnetic force produced by a short magnet.

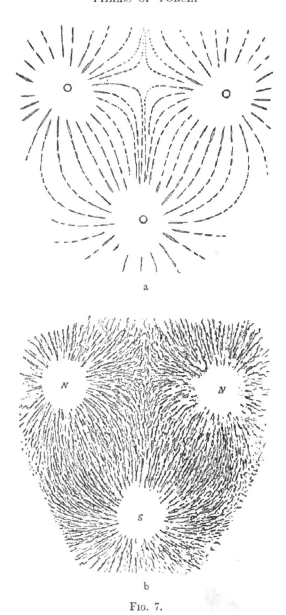

a

b

Fig. 7.

These figures show very fully the analogy in the geometry of the fields produced, on the one hand, by magnetic poles or magnets in a surrounding homogeneous medium, and, on the other hand,

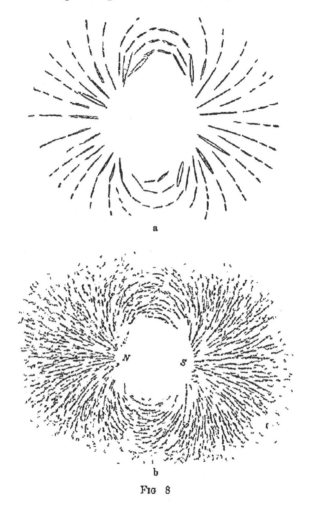

a

b

Fig 8

by pulsating or oscillating bodies in a surrounding homogeneous fluid   The experimental demonstration of the analogy for the case

when the medium surrounding the magnets and the fluid surrounding the pulsating or oscillating bodies contain heterogeneities is more
delicate   In the hydrodynamic case the heterogeneities should be
fluid, and it is practically impossible, on account of the action of
gravity, to have a fluid mass of given shape flowing freely in a
fluid of other density   If for the fluid bodies we substitute rigid
bodies, suspended from above or anchored from below, according to
their density, it is easily seen by means of our registering device,
that the lines of oscillation have a tendency to converge toward the
light, and to diverge from the heavy bodies   But this registering
device cannot be brought sufficiently near these bodies to show
the curves in their immediate neighborhood   Here the observation of the oscillations of small suspended particles would probably
be the best method to employ   Experiments which we shall perform later will give, however, indirect proofs that the fields have
exactly the expected character

16 *On Possible Extensions of the Analogy* — We have thus
found, by elementary reasoning, a very complete analogy between
the geometric properties of hydrodynamic fields and electric or
magnetic fields for the case of *statical* phenomena   And, to some
extent, we have verified these results by experiments

It is a natural question then, does the analogy extend to fields
of greater generality, or to fields of electromagnetism of the most
general nature? In discussing this question further an introduc-
tory remark is important   The formal analogy which exists between electrostatic and magnetic fields has made it possible for
us to compare the hydrodynamic fields considered with both electrostatic and magnetic fields   If there exists a perfect hydrodynamic analogy to electromagnetic phenomena, the hydrodynamic
fields considered will, presumably, turn out to be analogous either
to electrostatic fields only, or to magnetic fields only, but not to
both at the same time·   The question therefore can now be raised,
would our hydrodynamic fields in an eventually extended analogy
correspond to the electrostatic or the magnetic fields? To this it
must be answered, it is very probable that only the analogy to the

electrostatic fields will hold. As an obvious argument, it may be
emphasized that the hydrodynamic fields have exactly the generality of electrostatic fields, but greater generality than magnetic
fields. The analogy to magnetism will take the right form only
when the restriction is introduced, that changes of volume are to be
excluded. Otherwise, we should arrive at a theory of magnetism
where isolated magnetic poles could exist. To this argument
others may be added later.

But in spite of this, the formal analogy of the electric and magnetic fields makes it possible to formally compare hydrodynamic
fields with magnetic fields. And this will often be preferable, for
practical reasons. This will be the case in the following discussion, because the idea of the electric current is much more familiar
to us than the idea of the magnetic current, in spite of the formal
analogy of these two currents.

Let us compare, then, the hydrodynamic fields hitherto considered with magnetic fields produced by steel magnets. The lines of
force of these fields always pass through the magnets which produce
them, just as the corresponding hydrodynamic curves pass through
the moving bodies which produce the motion. The magnetic lines
of force produced by electric currents, on the other hand, are generally closed in the exterior space, and need not pass at all through
the conductors carrying the currents. To take a simple case, the
lines of force produced by an infinite rectilinear current are circles
around the current as an axis.

If it should be possible to extend the analogy so as to include
also the simplest electromagnetic fields, we would have to look for
hydrodynamic fields with closed lines of flow which do not pass
through the bodies producing the motion. It is easily preconceived, that if the condition of the oscillatory nature of the fluid
motion be insisted upon, the required motion cannot be produced by fluid pressure in a perfect fluid. A cylinder, for
instance, making rotary oscillations around its axis will produce
no motion at all in a perfect fluid. Quite the contrary is true,
if the fluid be viscous, or if it have a suitable transverse elasticity,

4

as does an aqueous solution of gelatine. But, as we shall limit ourselves to the consideration of perfect fluids, we shall not consider the phenomena in such media.

17. *Detached Hydrodynamic Analogy to the Fields of Stationary Electromagnetism.*—A direct continuation of our analogy is thus made impossible. It is a very remarkable fact, however, that there exist hydrodynamic fields which are geometrically analogous to the fields of stationary electric currents. But to get these fields we must give up the condition, usually insisted upon, that the motion be of oscillatory nature. We thus arrive at an independent analogy, which has a considerable interest in itself, but which is no immediate continuation of that considered above.

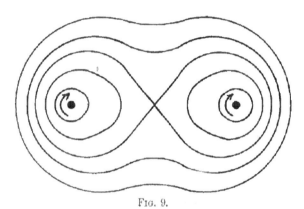

Fig. 9.

This analogy is that discovered by v. HELMHOLTZ in his research on the vortex motion of perfect fluids. According to his celebrated results, a vortex can be compared with an electric current, and the fluid field surrounding the vortex will then be in exactly the same relation to the vortex as the magnetic field is to the electric current which produces it.

To consider only the case of rectilinear vortices, the field of one rectilinear vortex is represented by concentric circles. And this field corresponds to the magnetic field of a rectilinear current. The hydrodynamic field of two rectilinear parallel vortices which have the same direction of rotation is shown in Fig. 9, and this field is strictly analogous to the magnetic field of two rectilinear parallel currents in the same direction. Fig. 10 gives the hydrodynamic field of two rectilinear parallel vortices which have opposite directions of rotation, and it is strictly analogous to the magnetic field of two electric currents of opposite direction.

Fields of this nature can be easily produced in water by rotating rigid cylinders, and observed by the motion of suspended particles. At the same time, each cylinder forms an obstruction in the field produced by the other. If only one cylinder be rotating,

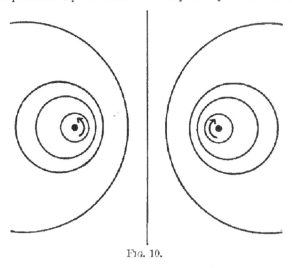

Fig. 10.

the lines of flow produced by it will be deflected so that they run tangentially to the surface of the other. The cylinder at rest thus influences the field just as a cylinder of infinite diamagnetivity would influence the magnetic field. The rotating cylinders therefore correspond to conductors for electric currents, which are constructed in a material of infinite diamagnetivity.

This analogy to electromagnetism is limited in itself, apart from its divergence from the analogy considered previously. The extreme diamagnetivity of the bodies is one limitation. Another limitation follows from Helmholtz's celebrated theorem, that vortices do not vary in intensity. Therefore phenomena corresponding to those of electromagnetic induction are excluded.

Whichever view we take of the subject, the hydrodynamic analogies to electric and magnetic phenomena are thus limited in extent. To get analogies of greater extent it seems necessary to pass to media with other properties than those of perfect fluids. But we will not try on this occasion to look for further extensions of the geometric analogies. We prefer to pass to an examination of the dynamic properties of the fields whose geometric properties we have investigated.

II.

ELEMENTARY INVESTIGATION OF THE DYNAMICAL PROPERTIES OF HYDRODYNAMIC FIELDS.

1. *The Dynamics of the Electric or the Magnetic Field.* — Our knowledge of the dynamics of the electric or magnetic field is very incomplete, and will presumably remain so as long as the true nature of the fields is unknown to us.

What we know empirically of the dynamics of the electric or magnetic field is this—bodies in the fields are acted upon by forces which may be calculated when we know the geometry of the field. Under the influence of these forces the bodies may take visible motions. But we have not the slightest idea of the hidden dynamics upon which these visible dynamic phenomena depend.

FARADAY's idea, for instance, of a tension parallel to, and a pressure perpendicular to the lines of force, as well as MAXWELL's mathematical translation of this idea, is merely hypothetical. And even though this idea may contain more or less of the truth, investigators have at all events not yet succeeded in making this dynamical theory a central one, from which all the properties of the fields, the geometric, as well as the dynamic, naturally develop, just as, for example, all properties of hydrodynamic fields, the geometric, as well as the dynamic, develop from the hydrodynamic equations. MAXWELL himself was very well aware of this incompleteness of his theory, and he stated it in the following words:

"It must be carefully born in mind that we have only made one step in the theory of the action of the medium. We have supposed it to be in a state of stress but have not in any way accounted for this stress, or explained how it is maintained. . . .

"I have not been able to make the next step, namely, to ac-

29

count by mechanical considerations for these stresses in the dielectric."

In spite of all formal progress in the domain of MAXWELL'S theory, these words are as true to-day as they were when MAXWELL wrote them. This circumstance makes it so much the more interesting to enter into the dynamic properties of the hydrodynamic fields, which have shown such remarkable analogy in their geometric properties to the electric or magnetic fields, in order to see if with the analogy in the geometric properties there will be associated analogies in their dynamical properties. The question is simply this:

Consider an electric, or magnetic field and the geometrically corresponding hydrodynamic field. Will the bodies which produce the hydrodynamic field, namely, the pulsating or the oscillating bodies or the bodies which modify it, such as bodies of other density than the surrounding fluid, be subject to forces similar to those acting on the corresponding bodies in the electric or magnetic fields?

This question can be answered by a simple application of the principle of kinetic buoyancy.

2. *Resultant Force against a Pulsating Body in a Synchronously Oscillating Current.* — Let us consider a body in the current produced by any system of synchronously pulsating and oscillating bodies. It will be continually subject to a kinetic buoyancy proportional to the product of the acceleration of the fluid masses into the mass of water displaced by it. If its volume be constant, so that the displaced mass of water is constant, the force will be strictly periodic, with a mean value zero in the period. It will then be brought only into oscillation, and no progressive motion will result.

But if the body has a variable volume, the mass of water displaced by it will not be constant. If the changes of volume consist in pulsations, synchronous with the pulsations, or oscillations, of the distant bodies which produce the current, the displaced mass of water will have a maximum when the acceleration has its maximum in one direction, and a minimum when the acceleration has its maximum in the opposite direction As is seen at once, the force can then no longer have the mean value zero in the period It will have a mean value in the direction of the acceleration at the time when the pulsating body has its maximum volume We thus find the result

A pulsating body in a synchronously oscillating current is subject to the action of a resultant force, the direction of which is that of the acceleration in the current at the time when the pulsating body has its maximum volume

3 *Mutual Attraction and Repulsion between Two Pulsating Bodies —*As a first application of this result, we may consider the case of two synchronously pulsating bodies Each of them is in the radial current produced by the other, and we have only to examine the direction of the acceleration in this current Evidently, this acceleration is directed outwards when the body producing it has its minimum volume, and is therefore about to expand, and is directed inwards when the body producing it has its maximum volume, and is therefore about to contract

Let us consider first the case of two bodies pulsating in the same phase They have then simultaneously their maximum volumes, and the acceleration in the radial current produced by the one body will thus be directed inwards, as regards itself, when the other body has its maximum volume The bodies will therefore be driven towards each other, there will be an apparent mutual attraction If, on the other hand, the bodies pulsate in opposite phase, one will have its maximum volume when the other has its minimum volume And therefore one will have its maximum volume when the radial acceleration is directed outward from the other The result, therefore, will be an apparent mutual repulsion

As the force is proportional to the acceleration in the radial current, and as the acceleration will decrease exactly as the velocity, proportionally to the inverse square of the distance, the force itself will also vary according to this law On the other hand, it is easily seen that the force must also be proportional to two parameters, which measure in a proper way the intensities of the pulsations of each body. Calling these parameters the "intensities of pulsation," we find the following law

Between bodies pulsating in the same phase there is an apparent attraction, between bodies pulsating in the opposite phase there is an apparent repulsion, the force being proportional to the product of the two intensities of pulsation, and proportional to the inverse square of the distance

4 *Discussion*—We have thus deduced from the principle of dynamic buoyancy, that is from our knowledge of the dynamics of the hydrodynamic field, that there will be a force which moves the pulsating bodies through the field, just as there exists, for reasons unknown to us, a force which moves a charged body through the electric field. And the analogy is not limited to the mere existence of the force. For the law enunciated above has exactly the form of COULOMB's law for the action between two electrically charged particles, with one striking difference, the direction of the force in the hydrodynamic field is opposite to that of the corresponding force in the electric or magnetic field. For bodies pulsating in the same phase must be compared with bodies charged with electricity of the same sign, and bodies pulsating in the opposite phase must be compared with bodies charged with opposite electricities. This follows inevitably from the geometrical analogy. For bodies pulsating in the same phase produce a field of the same geometrical configuration as bodies charged with the same electricity (Fig 5, *a* and *b*), and bodies pulsating in opposite phase produce the same field as bodies charged with opposite electricities (Fig 6, *a* and *b*)

This exception in the otherwise complete analogy is most astonishing. But we cannot discover the reason for it in the present limited state of our knowledge. We know very well why the force in the hydrodynamic field must have the direction indicated —this is a simple consequence of the dynamics of the fluid. But in our total ignorance of the internal dynamics of the electric or magnetic field we cannot tell at all why the force in the electric field has the direction which it has, and not the reverse

Thus, taking the facts as we find them, we arrive at the result that with the geometrical analogy developed in the preceding lecture there is associated an *inverse* dynamical analogy :

Pulsating bodies act upon each other as if they were electrically charged particles or magnetic poles, but with the difference that charges or poles of the same sign attract, and charges or poles of opposite sign repel each other.

5. *Pulsation Balance.*—In order to verify this result by experiment an arrangement must be found by which a pulsating body has a certain freedom to move. This may be obtained in different ways. Thus a pulsator may be suspended as a pendulum by a long india-rubber tube through which the air from the generator is brought. Or it may be inserted in a torsion balance, made of glass or metal tubing, and suspended by an india-rubber tube which brings the air from the generator and at the same time serves as a torsion wire. These simple arrangements have at the same time the advantage that they allow rough quantitative measurements of the force to be made. For good qualitative demonstrations the following arrangement will generally be found preferable.

The air from the generator comes through the horizontal metal tube, a, (Fig. 11), which is fixed in a support. The air channel continues vertically through the metal piece b, which has the form of a cylinder with vertical axis. At the top of this metal piece and in the axis there is a conical hole, and the lower surface is spherical with this hole as center. The movable part of the instrument rests on an adjustable screw, pivoted in this hole. This screw carries, by means of the arm d, the little cylinder c, through which the vertical air channel continues. The upper surface of this cylinder is spherical, with the point of the screw as center. The two spherical surfaces never touch each other, but by adjustment of the screw they may be brought so near each other that no sensible loss of air takes place. To the part of the instrument c–d, which gives freedom of motion, the pulsator may be connected by the tube $e\,f$, the counter-weight maintaining the equilibrium. By this arrangement, the pulsating body is free to move on a spherical

5

surface with the pivot as center, and the equilibrium will be neutral for a horizontal motion, and stable for a vertical motion.

6. *Experiments with Pulsating Bodies.*—Having one pulsator in the pulsation balance, take another in the hand, and arrange the

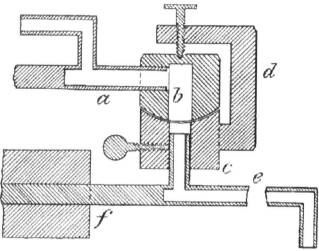

FIG. 11.

generator for pulsations of the same phase, and we see at once that the two pulsating bodies attract each other (Fig. 12, *a*). This attraction is easily seen with distances up to 10–15 cm., or more, and it is observed that the intensity of the force increases rapidly

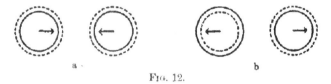

FIG. 12.

as the distance diminishes. The moment the relative phase of the pulsations is changed, the attraction ceases, and an equally intense repulsion appears (Fig. 12, *b*). With the torsion balance it may

be shown with tolerable accuracy, that the force varies as the inverse square of the distance, and is proportional to two parameters,
the intensities of pulsation.

In this experiment the mean value only of the force and the
progressive motion produced by it are observed. By using very
slow pulsations with great amplitudes, a closer analysis of the phenomenon is possible. It is then seen that the motion is not a
simple progressive one, but a dissymmetric vibratory motion, in
which the oscillations in the one direction always exceed a little
the oscillations in the other, so that the result is the observed
progressive motion.

7. *Action of an Oscillating Body upon a Pulsating Body.* —
Two oppositely pulsating bodies produce geometrically the same
field as two opposite magnetic poles. Geometrically, the field is
that of an elementary magnet. Into the field of these two oppositely pulsating bodies we can bring a third pulsating body.
Then, if we bring into application the law just found for the
action between two pulsating bodies, we see at once that the third
pulsating body will be acted upon by a force, opposite in direction to the corresponding force acting on a magnetic pole in
the field of an elementary magnet. In this result nothing will
be changed, if, for the two oppositely pulsating bodies, we substitute
an oscillating body. For both produce the same field, and the
action on the pulsating body will evidently depend only upon the
field produced, and not upon the manner in which it is produced.
We thus find :

*An oscillating body will act upon a pulsating body as an ele-
mentary magnet upon a magnetic pole, but with the law of poles
reversed.*

This result may be verified at once by experiment. If we take
an oscillator in the hand, and bring it near the pulsator which is
inserted in the pulsation-balance, we find attraction in the case
(Fig. 13, *a*) when the oscillating body approaches the pulsating
body as it expands and recedes from it as it contracts. But as
soon as the oscillating body is turned around, so that it approaches

while the pulsating body is contracting and recedes while it is expanding (Fig. 13, *b*), the attraction changes to repulsion.

To show how the analogy to magnetism goes even into the smallest details the oscillating body may be placed in the prolongation of the arm of the pulsation-balance, so that its axis of oscillation is perpendicular to this arm. The pulsating body will then move a little to one side and come into equilibrium in a dissymmetric position on one side of the attracting pole (Fig. 13, *c*). If the oscillating body be turned around, the position of equilibrium will be on the other side. Exactly the same small

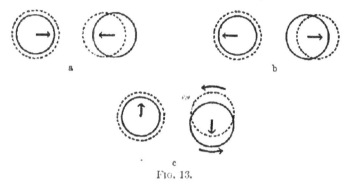

Fig. 13.

lateral displacement is observed when a short magnet is brought into the transverse position in the neighborhood of the pole of a long bar magnet which has the same freedom to move as the pulsating body.

8. *Force against an Oscillating Body.* — If, in the preceding experiment, we take the pulsating body in the hand and insert the oscillating body in the balance, we cannot conclude *a priori* that the motions of the oscillating body will prove the existence of a force equal and opposite to that exerted by the oscillating body upon the pulsating body. The principle of equal action and reaction is empirically valid for the common actions at a distance between two bodies. But for these *apparent* actions at a distance, where not only the two bodies but also a third one, the fluid, are engaged, no general conclusion can be drawn.

To examine the action to which the oscillating body is subject we must therefore go back to the principle of kinetic buoyancy. The kinetic buoyancy will give no resultant force against a body of invariable volume, which oscillates between two places in the fluid where the motion is the same. For at both ends of the path the body will be subject to the action of equal and opposite forces. But if it oscillates between places where the motion is somewhat different in direction and intensity, these two forces will not be exactly equal and opposite. The direction of the accelerations in the oscillating fluid masses is always tangential to the lines of oscillation. If the field be represented by these lines, and if the absolute value of the acceleration be known at every point of the fluid at any time, the force exerted on the oscillating body at every point of its path may be plotted, and the average value found. As we desire only qualitative results, it will be sufficient to consider the body in the two extreme positions only, where we have to do with the extreme values of the force.

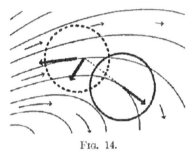

FIG. 14.

Let, then, the continuous circle (Fig. 14) represent the oscillating body in one extreme position, and the dotted circle the same body in the other extreme position, and let the two arrows be proportional to the accelerations which the fluid has at these two places at the corresponding times. The composition of these two alternately acting forces gives the average resultant force. Let us now substitute for the oscillating body a couple of oppositely pulsating bodies, one in each extreme position of the oscillating body, and let us draw arrows representing the average forces to which these two pulsating bodies are subject. We then get arrows located exactly as in the preceding case. And we conclude, therefore, that if we only adjust the intensities of pulsation properly, the

two oppositely pulsating bodies will be acted upon by exactly the
same average resultant force as the oscillating body. From the
results found above for the action against pulsating bodies we can
then conclude at once:

*An oscillating body in the hydrodynamic field will be subject to the
action of a force similar to that acting upon an elementary magnet
in the magnetic field, the only difference being the difference in the
signs of the forces which follows from the opposite pole-law.*

9. *Experimental Investigation of the Force exerted by a Pulsating Body upon an Oscillating Body.* — Let us now insert the
oscillator in the balance, and turn it so that the axis of oscillation
is in the direction of its free movement. If a pulsator be taken
in the hand, it will be seen that attraction takes place when the
pulsating body is made to approach one pole of the oscillating
body (Fig. 13, *a*), and repulsion if it is made to approach the
other pole (Fig. 13, *b*). And, as is evident from comparison with
the preceding case, the force acting on the oscillating body is always opposite to that acting on the pulsating body. We have
equality of action and reaction, just as in the case of magnetism.

The analogy with magnetism can be followed further if the
pulsating body be brought into the prolonged arm of the oscillation balance. The oscillating body will then take a short lateral
displacement, so that its attracting pole comes nearer to the pulsating body (Fig. 13, *c*). It is a lateral displacement corresponding exactly to that take by an elementary magnet under the influence of a magnetic pole.

10. *Experimental Investigation of the Mutual Actions between
Two Oscillating Bodies.* — The pulsator held in the hand may now
be replaced by an oscillator, while the oscillator inserted in the
balance is left unchanged, so that it is still free to move along its
axis of oscillation. We may first bring the oscillator held in the
hand into the position indicated by the figures 15, *a* and *b*, so that
the axes of oscillation lie in the same line. The experiment will
then correspond to that with magnets in longitudinal position. We
get attraction in the case, (Fig. 15, *a*), when the oscillating bodies

are in opposite phase. This corresponds to the case in which the magnets have poles of the same sign turned towards each other. If the oscillator held in the hand be turned around, so that the two bodies are in the same phase, the result will be repulsion (Fig. 15, *b*), while the corresponding magnets, which have opposite poles facing each other, will attract each other. Finally, the oscillator may be brought into the position (Fig. 15, *e*) in which it oscillates in the direction of the prolonged arm of the oscillation-

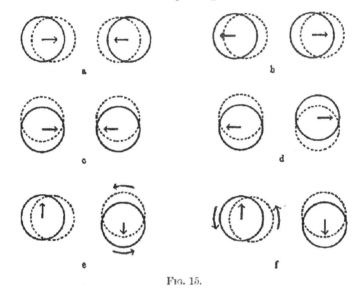

FIG. 15.

balance. Then we shall again get the small lateral displacement, which brings the attracting poles of the two oscillating bodies near each other.

The oscillator in the balance may now be turned around 90°, so that its oscillation is at right angles to the direction in which it is free to move. If both bodies oscillate normally to the line joining them, we get attraction when the bodies oscillate in the same phase (Fig. 15, *c*), and repulsion when they oscillate in the opposite phase (Fig. 15, *d*). This corresponds to the attraction and repulsion between parallel magnets, except that the direction of the force is, as usual, the reverse, the magnets repelling in the case of similar, and attracting in the case of opposite parallelism. If, finally, we place the oscillator in the prolonged arm of the balance with its axis of oscillation perpendicular to this arm (Fig. 15, *f*), we again get the small lateral displacement described above, exactly as with magnets in the corresponding positions, but in the opposite direction.

We have considered here only the most important positions of the two oscillating bodies and of the corresponding magnets. Between these principal positions, which are all distinguished by certain properties of symmetry, there is an infinite number of dissymmetric positions. In all of them it is easily shown that the force inversely corresponds to that between two magnets in the corresponding positions.

11. *Rotations of the Oscillating Body.* — We have considered hitherto only the resultant *force* on the oscillating body. But in general the two forces acting at the two extreme positions also form a *couple*, like the two forces acting on the two poles of a magnet. The first effect of this couple is to rotate the axis of oscillation of the body. But if this axis of oscillation has a fixed direction in the body, as is the case in our experiments, the body, will be obliged to follow the rotation of the axis of oscillation.

To show the effect of this couple experimentally the oscillator may be placed directly in the cylinder *c* (Fig. 11) of the pulsation-balance. It is then free to turn about a vertical axis passing through the pivot. If a pulsating body be brought into the neighborhood of this oscillating body, it immediately turns about its axis until the position of greatest attraction is reached, and as a consequence of its inertia it will generally go through a series of oscillations about this position of equilibrium. If the phase of the pulsations be changed, the oscillating body will turn around until its other pole comes as near as possible to the pulsating body. Apart from the direction of the force, the phenomena is exactly the analogue of a suspended needle acted upon by a magnetic pole.

The pulsating body may now be replaced by an oscillating body.

Except for the direction of the force, we shall get rotations corresponding to those of a compass needle under the influence of a magnet   The position of equilibrium is always the position of greatest attraction (Fig 15, a, c), the position of greatest repulsion being a position of unstable equilibrium   If the fixed oscillating body oscillates parallel to the line drawn from its center to that of the body in the balance, the position of stable equilibrium will be that indicated in Fig 16, b, and if it oscillates at right angles to this line, it will be the position indicated in Fig 16, d, while the intermediate dissymmetric positions of the fixed oscillator give intermediate dissymmetric positions of equilibrium of the movable oscillating body   It is easily verified that the posi-

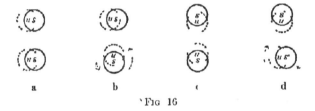

a   b   c   d

'Fig 16

tions of equilibrium are exactly the same as for the case of two magnets, except for the difference which is a consequence of the opposite pole-law ; the position of stable equilibrium in the magnetic experiment is a position of unstable equilibrium in the hydrodynamic experiment, and vice versa

12 *Forces Analogous to Those of Temporary Magnetism* — We have already considered the forces between bodies which are themselves the primary cause of the field, namely the bodies which have forced pulsations or oscillations   But, as we have shown, bodies which are themselves neutral but which have another density than that of the fluid also exert a marked influence upon the configuration of the field, exactly analogous to that exerted by bodies of different inductivity upon the configuration of the electric field   This action of the bodies upon the geometrical configuration of the field is, in the case of electricity or mag-

6

netism, accompanied by a mechanical force exerted by the field upon the bodies. We shall see how it is in this respect in the hydrodynamic field.

As we concluded from the principle of kinetic buoyancy, a body which is lighter than the water is brought into oscillation with greater amplitudes than those of the water; a body of the same density as the water will be brought into oscillation with exactly the same amplitude as the water; and a body which has greater density than the water will be brought into oscillation with smaller amplitudes than those of the water. From this we conclude that during the oscillations the body of the same density as the water will be always contained in the same mass of water. But both the light and the heavy body will in the two extreme positions be in different masses of water, and if these have not exactly

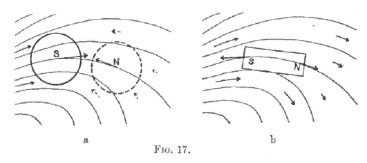

FIG. 17.

the same motion, it will be subject in these two positions to kinetic buoyancies not exactly equal and not exactly opposite in direction. The motion cannot therefore be strictly periodic. As a consequence of a feeble dissymmetry there will be superposed upon the oscillation a progressive motion.

That the average force which produces this progressive motion is strictly analogous to the force depending upon induced magnetism or electrification by influence, is easily seen. As we have already shown in the preceding lecture, the induced oscillations correspond exactly to the induced states of polarization in the electric or the magnetic field. Further, the forces acting in the two extreme positions of oscillation are in the same relation to the geometry of the field as the forces acting on the poles of the induced magnets, they are directed along the lines of force of the field, and vary in intensity from place to place according to the same law in the two kinds of fields, except that the direction of the force is always opposite in the two cases. Fig 17, *a* shows these forces in the two extreme positions of a light body, which oscillates with greater amplitudes than the fluid, and Fig 17, *b* shows the corresponding forces acting on the two poles of a magnetic body. Therefore, in the hydrodynamic field, the light body will be subject to a force oppositely equivalent to that to which the magnetic body in the corresponding magnetic field is subject. Fig 18, *a* shows the forces acting on the heavy body in its two extreme positions, the oscillations represented in the figure being those which it makes *relatively* to the

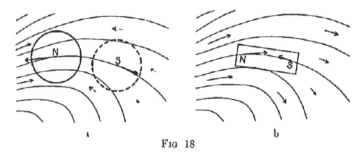

Fig 18

fluid, which is *the* oscillation which brings it into water masses with different motions. Fig 18, *b* shows the corresponding forces acting on the poles of an induced magnet of diamagnetic polarity. And, as is evident at once from the similarity of these figures, the heavy body in the hydrodynamic field will be acted upon by a force which oppositely corresponds to the force to which a diamagnetic body is subject in the magnetic field.

The well known laws for the motion of magnetic and diamagnetic bodies in the magnetic field can, therefore, be transferred at once to the motion of the light and heavy bodies in the hydrodynamic field. The most convenient of these laws is that of

FARADAY, which connects the force with the absolute intensity, or to the energy, of the field. Remembering the reversed direction of the force, we conclude that :

The light body will move in the direction of decreasing, the heavy body in the direction of increasing energy of the field.

13. *Attraction and Repulsion of Light and Heavy Bodies by a Pulsating or an Oscillating Body.* — If the field be produced by only one pulsating or one oscillating body, the result is very simple. For the energy of the field has its maximum at the surface of the pulsating or oscillating body, and will always decrease with increasing distance. Therefore, the light body will be repelled, and the heavy body attracted by the pulsating or the oscillating body.

To make this experiment we suspend in the water from a cork floating on the surface a heavy body, say a ball of sealing wax. In a similar manner we may attach a light body by a thread to a sinker, which either slides with a minimum pressure along the bottom of the tank, or which is itself held up in a suitable manner by corks floating on the surface. It is important to remark that the light body should never be fastened directly to the sinker, but by a thread of sufficient length to insure freedom of motion.

On bringing a pulsator up to the light body, it is seen at once to be repelled. If one is sufficiently near, the small induced oscillations of the light body may also be observed. If the pulsating body be brought near the heavy body, an attraction of similar intensity is observed. In both cases it is seen that the force decreases much more rapidly with the distance than in all the previous experiments, the force decreasing, as is easily proved, as the inverse fifth power of the distance, which is the same law of distance found for the action between a magnetic pole and a piece of iron.

If for the pulsating body we substitute an oscillating body, the same attractions and repulsions are observed. Both poles of the oscillating body exert exactly the same attraction on the heavy body, and exactly the same repulsion on the light body, and even the equatorial parts of the oscillating body exert the same attracting or repelling force, though to a less degree. As is easily seen we have also in this respect a perfect analogy to the action of a magnet on a piece of soft iron, or on a piece of bismuth.

14. *Simultaneous Permanent and Temporary Force* — As the force depending upon the induced pulsations, oscillations, or magnetizations, decreases more rapidly with increasing distance than the force depending upon the permanent pulsations, oscillations, or magnetizations, very striking effects may be obtained as the result of the simultaneous action of forces of both kinds. And these effects offer good evidence of the true nature of the analogy.

For one of the simplest magnetic experiments we can take a strong and a weak magnet, one of which is freely suspended. At a distance, the poles of the same sign will repel each other. But if they be brought sufficiently near each other, there will appear an attraction depending upon the induced magnetization. This induced magnetization is of a strictly temporary nature, for the experiment may be repeated any number of times.

We can repeat the experiment using the pulsation-balance and two pulsators, giving them opposite pulsations but with very different amplitudes. At a distance, they will repel each other, but if they be brought sufficiently near together they will attract. It is the attraction of one body, considered as a neutral body heavier than the water, by another which has intense pulsations.

Many experiments of this nature, with a force changing at a critical point from attraction to repulsion, may be made, all showing in the most striking way the analogy between the magnetic and the hydrodynamic forces.

15. *Orientation of Cylindrical Bodies* — The most common method of testing a body with respect to magnetism or diamagnetism is to suspend a long narrow cylindrical piece of the body in the neighborhood of a sufficiently powerful electromagnet. The cylinder of the magnetic body then takes the longitudinal, and the cylinder of the diamagnetic body the transverse position.

The corresponding hydrodynamic experiment is easily made

The light cylinder is attached from below and the heavy cylinder from above, and on bringing near a pulsating or an oscillating body, it is seen at once that the light cylinder, which corresponds to the magnetic body, takes the transverse, and the heavy cylinder, which corresponds to the diamagnetic body, the longitudinal position.

16. *Neutral Bodies Acted Upon by Two or More Pulsating or Oscillating Bodies.* — The force exerted by two magnets on a piece of iron is generally not the resultant found according to the parallelogram-law from the two forces which each magnet would exert by itself if the other were removed. For the direction of the greatest increase or decrease of the energy in the field due to both magnets is in general altogether different from the parallelogram-resultant of the two vectors which give the direction of this increase or decrease in the fields of the two magnets separately. It is therefore not astonishing that we get results which are in the most striking contrast to the principle of the parallelogram of forces, considered, it must be emphasized, as a physical principle, not merely as a mathematical principle; *i. e.*, as a means of the abstract representation of one vector as the sum of two or more other vectors.

In this way we may meet with very peculiar phenomena, which have great interest here, because they are well suited to show how the analogy between hydrodynamic and magnetic phenomena goes even into the most minute details. We shall consider here only the simplest instance of a phenomenon of this kind.

Let a piece of iron be attached to a cork floating on the surface of the water. If a magnetic north pole be placed in the water a little below the surface, the piece of iron will be attracted to a point vertically above the pole. If a south pole be placed in the same vertical symmetrically above the surface, nothing peculiar is observed; the piece of iron is held in its position of equilibrium more strongly than before. But if the second pole be a north pole, the iron will seem to be repelled from the point where it had previously stable equilibrium. It will move out to some point on a circle, the diameter of which is about $\frac{7}{10}$ of the distance between the poles If the same experiment were made with a piece of bismuth and sufficiently strong magnetic poles, the force would be in every case the reverse. It would have unstable equilibrium in the central point between two poles of opposite sign, and would seem to be repelled from this point But if the two poles were of the same sign, the bismuth would seem to be attracted to the point which previously repelled it, and it would be drawn to this point from any point within the circle mentioned above On the circle itself it would have unstable equilibrium, and outside it would be repelled

These peculiar phenomena are at once understood if we remember that the central point between two poles of the same sign is a neutral point, where the energy of the field has a minimum (Fig 5, b), and that the bismuth must move towards this point, the iron from it

To make the corresponding hydrodynamic experiment two pulsators may be placed one vertically above the other, and a light body (Fig 19, a) or a heavy body (Fig 19, b) brought between them. Then if they pulsate in opposite phase, the light body will be repelled from, and the heavy body attracted to the central point between the two pulsating bodies But if the phase be changed, so that the two bodies pulsate in the same phase, the light body will be attracted to this central point from all points inside a circle whose diameter is about $\frac{7}{10}$ of the distance between the pulsating bodies At all points outside of this circle it will be repelled The heavy body, on the other hand, will be repelled from the center to some point on the circle, but attracted from any point outside the circle, so that it will be in stable equilibrium on the circle

17 *Mutual Reactions between Bodies with Induced Magnetizations or with induced Oscillations* — Besides the direct actions of magnets on a piece of soft iron, we have also actions between any two pieces of soft iron which are acted upon by a magnet. This is of special interest, because it is upon this that the formation of the representations of fields of force in the classical experiment with iron filings depends The iron filings lying in the same line of

force acquire poles of opposite sign facing each other, and therefore
chain together.   Iron filings lying near each other on a line normal to a line of force have, on the other hand, poles of the same
sign facing each other, and therefore the chains formed mutually
repel each other, so that they become separated by distinct inter-
vals.   It is worth mentioning that, if the same experiment could
be made with filings of a diamagnetic body, such as bismuth, the
chain would be formed in the same way.   For when the poles of

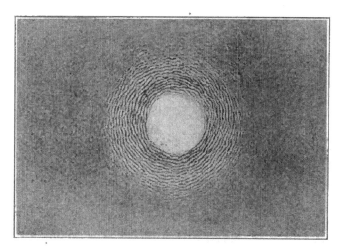

Fig. 19.

all the filings are changed at the same time, the direction of the
forces between them will be unchanged.

Similar actions will be observed between particles which take induced oscillations in the hydrodynamic field, except for the difference resulting from the direction of the force, which is opposite in
every case.   The particles, therefore, will chain together normally
to the lines of flow in the fluid; they will arrange themselves as
layers which follow the equipotential surfaces, and which, as a consequence of mutual repulsion, are separated from each other by
empty spaces.   It is indifferent whether for the experiment we

take a light powder, which would correspond to the iron filings, or
a heavy powder, which would correspond to the bismuth filings.

For practical reasons, it is preferable to use a heavy powder,
which, in order that the experiment succeed nicely, must be
fairly homogeneous. A good powder may be obtained from common red lead, if both the finest and the coarsest particles be removed by washing. This is distributed on a glass plate, directly
above which is placed for a few seconds a pulsating or an oscillating body with very intense pulsations or oscillations. The powder
immediately arranges itself along the expected curves.

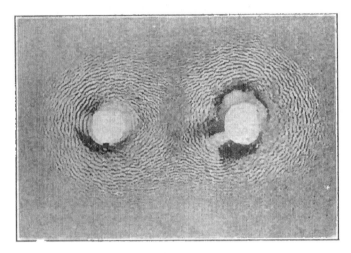

FIG. 20.

Fig. 19 gives the circles of a section through the spherical equipotential surfaces surrounding a pulsating body, and Figs. 20
and 21 give the more complicated curves of plane sections through
the equipotential surfaces produced by two bodies pulsating in the
same and in opposite phase, respectively. In a similar way Fig.
22 gives a section through the system of equipotential surfaces
around an oscillating body. As is easily seen, the curves thus
obtained are normal to the lines of force or of flow represented by
Figs. 4–8.

7

It is worth remarking that the dynamical principle which explains the formation of these figures is the same as that which explains the formation of KUNDT's dust-figures in the classical experiment for the measurement of the velocity of sound in gases. Our figures also show a striking likeness to the ripple marks formed in the sand along the shores by the waves. And even though the dynamical principle developed here does not fully account for the peculiarities of these ripple marks, especially when they have great dimensions, it is certainly the principle which accounts for

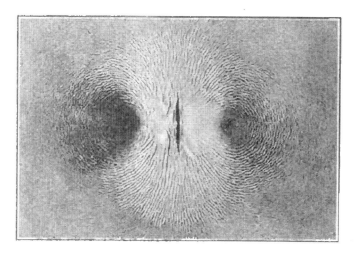

FIG. 21.

the beginning of their formation. The fossil ripple marks, which are well known to the geologists, then prove that the laws of hydrodynamic fields of force, which I develop before you in this lecture, were the same in previous geological periods as they are to-day.

18. *Vortices and Electric Currents.* — We have obtained the most complete analogy possible of hydrodynamic phenomena to the phenomena of electrostatics or of magnetism, the only difference being that depending upon the inverse pole-law.

Our investigation of the geometry of the field showed us

that we meet with difficulties if we try to extend the analogy beyond this point. The discovery of a complete dynamical analogy to the phenomena of electromagnetism therefore necessarily supposes a more or less complete modification of the views which have led us to the discovery of the partial analogy already developed. To prepare for a discovery of this kind we can hardly do better than to discuss the other conditions which lead to a partial analogy which is related to the analogy which we have developed, although it does not form an immediate continuation of it.

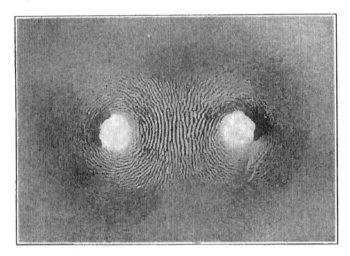

Fig. 22.

As we remarked when we discussed the geometry of the fields, there is an analogy, discovered by v. HELMHOLTZ, between the magnetic fields of electric currents and hydrodynamic fields depending upon vortex motion. This geometric analogy very nearly forms a continuation of the analogy with which we have been mostly occupied, the only reason why it cannot form a perfect continuation being that the fluid vortex must always go around in the same direction, so that a vortex of vibratory nature is impossible. But taking this analogy as it is, detached from the preceeding analogy, we will examine whether in this case also there exists an analogy between the dynamics of the two systems.

Let us first consider a rectilinear cylindrical vortex in the middle of a tank, which is itself at rest. The motion of circulation around the vortex, which corresponds to the magnetic field around the corresponding electric current, will be perfectly symmetrical. The distribution of the pressure will, therefore, also be symmetrical, and there will be no resultant force against the vortex. Nor will any such force appear if a common motion of translation be communicated to the tank and to the vortex. Otherwise it would be possible to discover by an experiment of this kind the motion of the earth.

But now let us suppose the motion of translation to be given to the tank only, while the vortex, or a rotating rigid cylinder substituted for the vortex, be held still. There will then be a dissymmetry in the distribution of the motion on the two sides of the rotating cylinder; on one side, the motion of translation will be added to, on the other side, subtracted from the motion of circulation around the cylinder. As we have in this case a stationary motion depending upon a potential, there will be in the fluid a diminution of the pressure proportional to the kinetic energy in the fluid motion, and therefore an excess of pressure on the side where there is a neutralization of the two motions. The cylinder, therefore, is driven transversely through the field, in the direction in which there is addition of the velocities. This corresponds exactly to the transverse motion of an electric current through a homogeneous magnetic field, but with the same difference of sign as before; the electric current is driven in the direction in which the field intensity due to the current is neutralized by that due to the homogeneous field.

The rectilinear cylindrical vortex which we have considered may now be an element of any vortex. Therefore we may draw this general conclusion; the elements of any vortex which is stationary in space, will, in the hydrodynamic field, be subject to a force oppositely corresponding to that to which the elements of the corresponding electric current are subject in the corresponding magnetic field. As special consequences, we deduce, for example, that parallel vortices which rotate in the same sense, and which correspond thus to currents of the same direction, will repel, while vortices rotating in the opposite direction will attract each other.

As is seen from this deduction, the condition that the vortices should be stationary in space is essential. If the elements of the vortices participate in the motion of the surrounding field, we come back to the case where the rectilinear vortex had the same motion as the tank, and in this case there was no force. The analogy which we have found is therefore strictly limited to the case of stationary electromagnetism. Thus for two reasons this restriction is imposed upon the analogy. As we saw in the investigation of the geometry of the analogy, the constancy of the vortices makes hydrodynamic phenomena corresponding to the induction of currents impossible. Now we see that the mechanical forces have values analogous to those acting against the electric currents, only when the vortices which correspond to the electric currents are perfectly stationary in space. The analogy, therefore, is a limited one; but even in its limited state it may give us suggestions.

19. *Experiments with Rotating Cylinders.* —Simple cases of the results developed may easily be tested experimentally. By means of turbines driven by air-jets, we may set metal cylinders into rotation, which in turn produce the required circulation of the surrounding water masses in consequence of friction. One such cylinder may be held in the hand by means of a suitable support. Another may be introduced into the instrument previously used as a pulsation- or oscillation-balance. It is necessary, however, in order to prevent the cylinder in the balance from taking by itself a translatory motion through the fluid, always to use two oppositely rotating cylinders which are arranged symmetrically about a vertical axis through the pivot (Fig. 23).

With this instrument, it is easily shown that cylinders rotating in the same direction repel, and that cylinders rotating in the opposite direction attract.

We have observed also that a non-rotating cylinder effects the configuration of the hydrodynamic field, just as a cylinder of

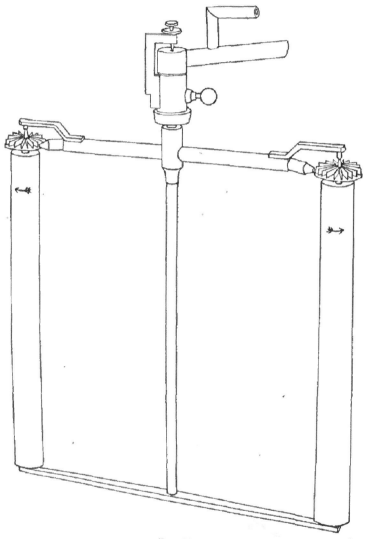

Fig. 23.

infinite diamagnetivity effects the magnetic field (1, 16) Even this geometric analogy is accompanied with an inverse dynamic analogy, it is easily seen that the rotating and the resting cylinder attract each other, just as a wire, carrying an electric current, and a diamagnetic body repel each other

III

THE GEOMETRIC PROPERTIES OF ELECTRO-MAGNETIC FIELDS ACCORDING TO MAXWELL'S THEORY.

1. *C. A. Bjerknes' Problems and Methods.*—All the phenomena investigated in the preceding lectures by elementary reasoning and experiment were found originally through mathematical analysis by the late Professor C. A. BJERKNES. While searching for phenomena of hydrodynamics which should have the appearance of actions at a distance, he solved the problem of the simultaneous motion of any number of spherical bodies in a liquid. The discussion of the solution led him to results which he verified later by a series of experiments, of which I have shown you the most important, using, however, instruments of improved construction.

We apparently deviate from the historical method in taking the elementary reasoning and experiment first and then proceeding to the mathematical theory. But this deviation may in some sense be more apparent than real. For the phenomena to be examined certainly had in the mind of the discoverer the form of ideal experiments long before their final mathematical solution was obtained. And the exact calculations were, in part, at least, preceded by elementary reasoning, which was not always correct perhaps and of which the greater part was lost after the exact mathematical solution was found. We may therefore have good reason to believe that, starting as we have done with elementary reasoning and experiment, we have in some sense restored the original method of the discoverer, improved according to our present exact knowledge of the subject.

2. *The Problem of Analogies.* — Proceeding now to the mathematical theory we shall also, in one sense, deviate considerably from

the original method followed by the discoverer   At the beginning the solution of the problem of spheres was certainly the most
natural way of submitting the vague anticipations to a rigorous
test, for this was the time when the theory of the action at a distance was predominant, and the discovery of the simplest and most
striking instances of *apparent* actions at a distance was the most
fascinating result for a man opposing this theory to strive for

But time has changed   The doctrine of action at a distance
has been given up, and it is the aim of no natural philosopher to
oppose it   The time of fields of force has come, and it is our aim
now to widen and deepen our knowledge of these fields   The
hydrodynamic phenomena discovered by C A BJERKNES were
field phenomena, and their analogy to electrical phenomena are
even still more striking according to our new views   But the
change of view also suggested a quite new method of developing
the results, with unexpected facility and generality   Of course, if
there exists a close analogy between hydrodynamic and electromagnetic fields, this analogy must be contained implicitly in the fundamental equations of the two kinds of fields, namely in the hydrodynamic equations of motion on the one hand, and in MAXWELL's
equations of the electromagnetic field on the other   And this is
exactly what I am going to show you, namely, that the analogy
may be developed directly from these two sets of equations

The method thus indicated is, indeed, perfectly plain and easy
There is no difficulty in finding the properties of hydrodynamic
fields, and the only real difficulty with which we meet arises from
the imperfection of our knowledge of electromagnetic fields.   To
lay the safest possible foundation for our research we have first to
analyze carefully our knowledge of these fields   This will be the
object of the lectures of to-day and to-morrow

3 *Maxwell's Theory* — Our knowledge of electromagnetic fields
is contained in what is generally called MAXWELL's theory   This
theory does not tell us what electromagnetic fields are in their true
nature   It is a formal theory, bearing upon two aspects of the
properties of the fields   What are generally called MAXWELL's

8

equations give a very full description of the variation from time
to time of the geometric configuration of electromagnetic fields.
To this geometric theory is only feebly linked the much less developed theory of the dynamical properties of these fields.

MAXWELL'S theory has a central core, generally called the
equations for the free ether, relating to which there is good
agreement among different writers.   But this agreement ceases
when we pass to the equations for ponderable bodies and for moving media, and, as will be seen, the full discussion of the analogy
will depend upon certain details of the theory for this general
case.   Proceeding to outline the theory, I shall follow principally
OLIVER HEAVISIDE,* whom I have found to be my safest guide
in this department of physics for several reasons, of which I will
emphasize two ; that he uses a perfectly rational system of units,
and that he takes into consideration more fully than other writers
the impressed forces, which play a great part, from a certain point
of view even the greatest part, in the theory to be developed.   But
instead of HEAVISIDE'S I shall use my own notation, chosen partly
to economize letters, partly that analogies and contrasts in the
things shall be reflected in analogies and contrasts in the
notation.

In thus outlining MAXWELL'S theory I wish to emphasize that
I do not introduce anything new.   What I introduce I have found
in other authors, who were perfectly uninfluenced by the search
for the hydrodynamic analogy.   The guarantee for an unprejudiced test of this analogy is, therefore, so far as I can see, perfect.

4. *Inductivity.* — To a material medium we attribute two constants, defining its specific properties in relation to the two kinds
of fields.   These two constants define, so to speak, the readiness
of the medium to let electric or magnetic lines of induction pass,
and may be called the electric inductivity, α, and the magnetic inductivity, β.

We do not know the exact nature of the properties defined by
these constants.   They can, therefore, not be determined in abso-

* Oliver Heaviside, Electromagnetic Theory.   Vol. I.   London, 1893.

lute measure   What we can measure are only their ratios for
any two media

$$\frac{\alpha}{\alpha_0}, \qquad \frac{\beta}{\beta_0}$$

If α_0 and β_0 be the constants of the free ether, these ratios are
called the specific inductive capacities, electric and magnetic
respectively, of the medium which has the inductivities α
and β

When we consider thus the properties of any medium in relation to the fields as defined by one electric and by one magnetic constant only, we limit ourselves to the consideration of strictly isotropic substances, which remain isotropic even when strained, as
is the case, for instance, with liquids   But any degree of heterogeneity may be allowed   These suppositions give to the fields
exactly the generality wanted for our purpose

5 *Electric and Magnetic Vectors* — We will consider in this
lecture the geometric description of electromagnetic fields   To give
this description, a series of special electric and special magnetic vectors has been introduced

We believe that these vectors represent real physical states existing in, or real physical processes going on in the medium which
is the seat of the field   But the nature of these states or processes
is perfectly unknown to us   What still gives them, relatively
speaking, a distinct physical meaning is, as we shall show more
completely in the next lecture, that certain expressions formed by
the use of these vectors represent quantities, such as energy, force,
activity, etc , in the common dynamical sense of these words
These quantities can be measured in absolute measure   But their
expressions as functions of the electric or magnetic vectors contain
always two quantities of unknown physical nature   When once
the discovery of a new law of nature allows us to write another
independent equation containing the same unknown quantities, we
shall be able to define perfectly the nature of the electric and magnetic vectors, and submit them to absolute measurements in the real
sense of this expression   Provisionally, we can only do exactly

the same as does the mathematician in problems where he has more unknowns than equations, viz., content ourselves with relative determinations, considering provisionally one or other of the unknown quantities as if it were known. But we retain the symbols for the unknown quantities in all formulæ bearing upon the pure theory of electromagnetic phenomena, for this will be the best preparation for the final solution of the problem.

This imperfect knowledge is, of course, also the reason why our theory of electromagnetic fields is split into two different, loosely connected, parts ; first, the geometric theory of the fields, where the relation of the vectors to time and space is considered independently of every question of the physical sense of the vectors ; and second, the dynamical theory of the fields, where the question of the nature of the vectors is taken up, but only imperfectly solved.

6. *Classification of the Vectors.* — The vectors introduced to describe the fields may be divided into classes differing from each other in their mathematical properties, or in the physical facts to which they relate.

On the one hand, the electric as well as the magnetic vectors are divided in two classes, designated generally as *forces* and *fluxes*. As the forces cannot be proved to have anything to do with forces in the classical dynamical sense of the word, a more neutral name will be preferable. I will therefore use the words *field intensities* and *fluxes*. Between field intensities and fluxes there is this relation : by the multiplication of a field intensity by the inductivity of the medium a corresponding flux is formed.

Field intensities and fluxes are vectors of different physical nature. They cannot therefore be added together. This is an important remark. For, according to previous imperfect views of the electromagnetic problem, this distinction was not made, and much confusion was caused by the lumping together of heterogeneous quantities. But in the case of electricity, as well as in magnetism, any two field intensities may be added together, likewise any two fluxes.

Taking now another point of view, we can divide the field intensities into *induced*, and *impressed* or *energetic field intensities*, and
the fluxes likewise into *induced*, and *impressed* or *energetic fluxes*

The theory of induced fluxes and field intensities we have to some
extent really mastered   MAXWELL's equations are the laws principally obeyed by these vectors.   But in order to complete the system formally, the impressed or energetic fluxes and field intensities
are introduced   They represent certain states, or processes, under
certain circumstances existing in, or going on in, the matter, and
which are ultimately the origin of every electric or magnetic phenomenon   The intrinsic polarization in the permanent magnet,
or in the pyroelectric crystal, is therefore represented by vectors
of this class   They are introduced further as auxiliary vectors
for the representation of the creation of electric energy by contact-
electricity, in the thermopile, or in the voltaic battery   As the
existence or the supply of electric or magnetic energy is related
ultimately to states or processes represented by these vectors, I
have termed them energetic vectors, a name given originally by C
A BJERKNES to the corresponding hydrodynamic vectors

From the fundamental vectors thus defined we may form new
ones by the addition of vectors of the same kind   Thus the addition of the induced and the energetic field intensities gives the
total or *actual* field intensities, and the addition of the induced and
the energetic flux gives the *total* or *actual* fluxes   We have thus
introduced six electric and six magnetic vectors   But in each
group of six vectors only two are really independent of each other,
and thus only two are really needed for the full description of the
electric or the magnetic field   Which pair of vectors it will be
convenient to choose as independent will depend upon the nature
of the problem to be treated   But a certain pair of vectors seems
in the majority of cases to turn out as the most convenient, this
is the *actual flux* and the *induced field intensity*   These we therefore distinguish beyond the others, calling them simply *the* flux,
and *the* field intensity, in every case when their qualities as actual
flux and induced field intensity need not be specially emphasized

7. *Notation.* — It is very convenient for our purpose to introduce such notation as to make it at once evident to which class or group the vector belongs. To attain this I denote fluxes with capitals and field intensities with the corresponding small letters. On the other hand, actual, induced, and energetic vectors are designated by the subscripts a, i, e, but with the exception that the letters designating *the* flux and *the* field intensity, according to the definitions above, are distinguished by the omission of subscripts. Finally, for the electric vectors I use the first, and for the magnetic vectors the second letter of the Latin alphabet, corresponding to the first and second letter of the Greek alphabet introduced above to represent the inductivities.

The system of notation is contained in the following scheme :

		Electric.		Magnetic.	
	Flux.	Field intensity.	Flux.	Field intensity.
(A)	Actual	A	a_a	B	b_a
	Induced	A_i	a	B_i	b
	Energetic	A_e	a_e	B_e	b_e

Electric inductivity α.   Magnetic inductivity β.

Between each group of six vectors there are, according to what is stated above, four relations, namely :

(a)
$$A = A_i + A_e, \qquad B = B_i + B_e,$$
$$a_a = a + a_e, \qquad b_a = b + b_e,$$
$$A_i = \alpha a, \qquad B_i = \beta b,$$
$$A_e = \alpha a_e, \qquad B_e = \beta b_e.$$

By different eliminations we can of course give different forms to these equations of connection. When we agree to use *the* flux and *the* field intensity as the fundamental vectors, we need the equations of connection, especially if vectors of the energetic group have to be introduced. As we prefer generally in such cases to introduce the energetic flux, we shall usually have to employ the following form of the equations of connection,

(b) $$A = \alpha a + A_e, \qquad B = \beta b + B_e$$

I am aware, of course, that the multiplication of systems of notation, already too numerous, may be objectionable But it will serve for my excuse, I hope, that suggestive notations are perhaps nowhere of greater importance than in researches of a comparative nature The question of a system of notation, at the same time simple and suggestive, with reference to the whole of theoretical physics, will, I think, necessarily arise sooner or later

8 *Conductivity, Time of Relaxation* — Besides their electric and magnetic inductivities, some or most media have still an intrinsic property, their electric conductivity The constant best suited to represent this property in the fundamental equations is the time of relaxation, introduced first by E. COHN If an electric field in a conducting medium be left to itself, its electric energy will be transformed into heat, and the electric field will disappear This may happen so that the configuration of the field is left unaltered during this process of relaxation The time in which the electric vector, during this process, diminishes to the fraction $1/e$ of its initial value (e being the base of the natural logarithms) is the relaxation time T This is a real intrinsic constant of the medium, measurable moreover in absolute measure, and therefore in theoretical researches to be preferred to the conductivity γ, to which it is related by the equation

(a) $$T = \frac{\alpha}{\gamma}$$

A corresponding magnetic conductivity and time of relaxation is not known It is convenient, however, in order to obtain a perfect symmetry of the formulæ, to introduce symbols even for these fictitious quantities, say κ for magnetic conductivity and T' for the corresponding time of relaxation

(b) $$T' = \frac{\beta}{\kappa}$$

9. *Integral Form of the Fundamental Laws.* — Using induced field intensity, actual, and energetic flux, we have always to remember first the equations of connection

(a)

$$A = \alpha a + A_e,$$
$$B = \beta b + B_s.$$

A set of cross connections between electric flux and magnetic field intensity, and *vice versa*, between magnetic flux and electric field intensity, is contained in the two "circuital" laws, to use HEAVISIDE's expression. To find the mathematical expressions of these laws we consider a surface bordered by a closed curve. In case the medium is moving, the surface should also move, following exactly the material particles with which it coincides at the beginning. To coordinate the positive side of the surface with the positive direction of circulation on the bordering curve we utilize the positive screw-rule. Denoting by r the radius vector from a fixed origin to a point of the closed curve, by dr the vector-line element of the curve, by ds the vector-surface element of the surface, the two circuital laws may be written

(b)

$$\frac{d}{dt}\int A \cdot ds + \int \frac{1}{T} A \cdot ds = \int b \cdot dr,$$
$$\frac{d}{dt}\int B \cdot ds + \int \frac{1}{T'} B \cdot ds = -\int a \cdot dr.$$

The sum of the surface integrals of the first equation is generally called the electric current through the surface, the first representing the displacement-current in the widest sense of this word, and the second the conduction current. In the same way the surface-integrals of the second equation represent the magnetic current, the second term, which represents the magnetic conduction-current, being merely fictitious. Utilizing these expressions, the core of our knowledge of the properties of electro-magnetic fields in relation to time and space may be expressed in the following propositions.

The electric current through a moving material surface equals the positive line integral of the magnetic field intensity round the border of the surface.

The magnetic current through a moving material surface equals the negative line integral of the electric field intensity round the border of the surface.

To these equations, containing the two fundamental laws, we have to add two equations containing the definition of two important auxiliary quantities, the electric and the magnetic mass, or equivalently, the electric and the magnetic density. Calling E the electric and M the magnetic density, then the electric or the magnetic mass contained within a closed surface is the volume integral respectively of E or M within the surface. These masses are defined as functions of the fluxes by the equations

(c)
$$\int E d\tau = \int \mathbf{A} \cdot d\mathbf{s}$$
$$\int M d\tau = \int \mathbf{B} \cdot d\mathbf{s},$$

$d\tau$ being the element of volume. Thus the mass within a surface is defined by the total flux through the surface.

It must be emphasized that these equations are, from our point of view, only equations of definition, not laws of nature. This assertion is not contradicted by the historical fact that the notion of masses was first introduced, and later the vectors defined by use of the masses, while we now consider the vectors as the fundamental quantities, and define the masses by the vectors. It seems to be an empirical fact, however, that no magnetic mass exists, and this assertion then contains a law of nature to which the magnetic flux is subject, and which limits the generality of the magnetic field. But for the sake of analytical generality and the advantages of a complete symmetry, it will be convenient to retain the symbol M for magnetic density in our formulæ.

To these fundamental equations a system of supplementary conditions is usually to be added. Thus, it is generally considered that the values of each inductivity, α and β, and the relaxation time T are known at all points of the field. The same supposition

9

is generally made for the energetic fluxes, and for the electric and magnetic densities. In the case of conductors a knowledge of the total electric mass only for each conductor is wanted. This sort of special knowledge is wanted only for material bodies, and not for the free ether. For it is generally admitted that here the inductivities have constant values, a_0, and β_0, that the relaxation-time is infinite, $1/T = 0$, and that energetic vectors and electric or magnetic densities do not exist, $\mathbf{A}_e = \mathbf{B}_s = 0$, $E = M = 0$. These conditions very much simplify the problems.

10. *Differential Form of the Fundamental Equations.* — From the integral forms above we can, by a well known mathematical process, pass to the differential form of the same equations, and thus arrive at the form of the system of electromagnetic equations generally most convenient for practical use.

The equations of connection of course retain their form

(a)
$$\mathbf{A} = a\mathbf{a} + \mathbf{A}_e,$$
$$\mathbf{B} = \beta\mathbf{b} + \mathbf{B}_e.$$

The equations expressing the two circuital laws may be written in the following simple forms,

(b_1)
$$\mathbf{c} = \operatorname{curl} \mathbf{b},$$
$$\mathbf{k} = -\operatorname{curl} \mathbf{a},$$

where the auxiliary quantities $\mathbf{c}$ and $\mathbf{k}$ are the electric and the magnetic current densities respectively, the full expressions for which are

(b_2)
$$\mathbf{c} = \frac{\partial \mathbf{A}}{\partial t} + \operatorname{curl}(\mathbf{A} \times \mathbf{V}) + (\operatorname{div} \mathbf{A})\mathbf{V} + \frac{1}{T}\mathbf{A},$$
$$\mathbf{k} = \frac{\partial \mathbf{B}}{\partial t} + \operatorname{curl}(\mathbf{B} \times \mathbf{V}) + (\operatorname{div} \mathbf{B})\mathbf{V} + \frac{1}{T'}\mathbf{B},$$

$\mathbf{V}$ being the velocity of the moving medium, and $\partial/\partial t$ the *local* time differentiator, which is related to the *individual* time differentiator used above by the Eulerian relation

(b_3)
$$\frac{d}{dt} = \frac{\partial}{\partial t} + \mathbf{V} \cdot \nabla.$$

The second equation contains two terms which represent merely fictitious quantities, namely, (div B) **V**, which represents the magnetic convection-current, and $1/T'$ **B**, which represents the magnetic conduction current

The equations of definition of the electric and magnetic densities finally take the form

(c)
$$E = \operatorname{div} \mathbf{A},$$
$$M = \operatorname{div} \mathbf{B}$$

To these fundamental relations we add the equations which give the special features of the free ether, namely,

(d)
$$\alpha = \alpha_0, \qquad \frac{1}{T} = 0, \qquad E = 0, \qquad \mathbf{A}_e = 0,$$
$$\beta = \beta_0, \qquad \frac{1}{T'} = 0, \qquad M = 0, \qquad \mathbf{B}_e = 0,$$

which are satisfied in all space outside the bodies

11 Stationary State. — The principal feature of electromagnetic fields, as expressed by the equations above, is this   every variation in time of an electric field is connected with the existence of a magnetic field of a certain geometric quality, and *vice versa.* every variation in time of a magnetic field is connected with the existence of an electric field of a certain geometric quality

This close cross connection of electric and magnetic phenomena is reduced to a feeble link in the case of stationary phenomena, and disappears completely when we pass to static phenomena To consider stationary fields, that is, fields which do not vary in time, let the medium be at rest, $\mathbf{V} = 0$, and let the vectors **A** and B have values which are at every point of space independent of the time   The expressions $(10, b_2)$ for the two current densities reduce to

(a)
$$c = \frac{1}{T'} \mathbf{A},$$
$$k = \frac{1}{T'} \mathbf{B}$$

The first of these equations is the most general expression for OHM's law for the conduction-current, which is thus the only current existing under stationary conditions. The second equation gives the corresponding law for the fictitious magnetic current. The currents are the quantities which connect the electric fields with the magnetic fields, and *vice versa*. But utilizing the invariability of the current, we can now simply consider the distribution of the currents in the conducting bodies as given, and thus treat the two stationary fields separately, without any reference to each other.

Writing the equations of the two stationary fields, we have

$$(b_1) \quad \begin{aligned} \mathbf{A} &= \alpha\mathbf{a} + \mathbf{A}_e, & \mathbf{B} &= \beta\mathbf{b} + \mathbf{B}_e, \\ \operatorname{curl} \mathbf{a} &= -\mathbf{k}, & \operatorname{curl} \mathbf{b} &= \mathbf{c}, \\ \operatorname{div} \mathbf{A} &= E, & \operatorname{div} \mathbf{B} &= M, \end{aligned}$$

where the current densities $\mathbf{c}$ and $\mathbf{k}$ are now among the quantities generally considered as given. To these fundamental equations the conditions for the free ether must be added. The condition that the free ether has no conductivity implies now that no current whatever exists in it; these conditions can be written

$$(b_2) \quad \begin{aligned} \alpha &= \alpha_0, & \beta &= \beta_0, \\ \mathbf{A}_e &= 0, & \mathbf{B}_e &= 0, \\ E &= 0, & M &= 0, \\ \mathbf{k} &= 0, & \mathbf{c} &= 0, \end{aligned}$$

for the two fields respectively.

Each of the two systems of equations contains one fictitious quantity. The equations for the electric field contain the stationary magnetic current density $\mathbf{k}$, and the equations for the electric field contain the density of magnetism M, both of which are fictitious.

12. *Static State.* — If, in the equations for stationary fields, we suppose the current density to be everywhere nil, we get the

equations for static fields,

$$A = \alpha a + A_e, \qquad B = \beta b + B_e,$$

(a_1)
$$\operatorname{curl} a = 0, \qquad \operatorname{curl} b = 0,$$

$$\operatorname{div} A = E, \qquad \operatorname{div} B = M,$$

with the conditions for the free ether,

$$\alpha = \alpha_0, \qquad \beta = \beta_0,$$

(b_2)
$$A_e = 0, \qquad B_e = 0,$$

$$E = 0, \qquad M = 0$$

These static fields exist independently of each other, the links which, in the general case, connect the one kind of field to the other, namely, the currents, being nil

13 *The Energy Integral* — A research relating to the completeness of the description which the preceding equations give of the geometry of the fields will be of fundamental importance in the search for the analogy of these fields to other fields   As an introduction to this research, we will examine from an analytical point of view an integral, the physical significance of which will occupy us in the next lecture, namely, the integral expressing the electric or the magnetic energy of the field

The expression for the electric energy can always be written

(a)
$$\Phi = \tfrac{1}{2} \int A \; a_a \, d\tau,$$

where the integration is extended to all space   Now in the case of perfect isotropy the actual field intensity is related to the flux simply by the relation

(b)
$$A = \alpha a_a,$$

and, therefore, we have the equivalent expressions for the energy

(c)
$$\Phi = \int \frac{1}{2\alpha} A^2 d\tau = \int \tfrac{1}{2} \alpha a_a^2 d\tau$$

Now let us write the vector-factor **A**, of the scalar product, in the form

$$\mathbf{A} = -\,\alpha\nabla\phi + \operatorname{curl}\mathbf{G},$$

expressing it thus by a scalar potential ϕ and a vector potential **G**, as is possible with any vector. The integral may then be written

$$\Phi = -\tfrac{1}{2}\int\mathbf{A}\cdot\nabla\phi\,d\tau + \int\tfrac{1}{2}\mathbf{a}_a\cdot\operatorname{curl}\mathbf{G}\,d\tau.$$

To avoid circumlocution we shall suppose that there exists in the field no real discontinuity, every apparent surface of discontinuity being in reality an extremely thin sheet, in which the scalars or the vectors of the field change their values at an exceedingly rapid rate, but always continuously. Further, we suppose that the field disappears at infinity. Both integrals can be transformed then according to well known formulæ, giving for the energy the new expression

(d) $$\Phi = \tfrac{1}{2}\int\phi\operatorname{div}\mathbf{A}\,d\tau + \tfrac{1}{2}\int\mathbf{G}\cdot\operatorname{curl}\mathbf{a}_a\,d\tau.$$

Now div **A** is the density of true electrification, which exists only in material bodies. It will be sufficient, therefore, to apply the first integral to material bodies only, and not to the surrounding ether. If we split the actual field intensity $\mathbf{a}_a$ into its induced and energetic parts, we get

$$\operatorname{curl}\mathbf{a}_a = \operatorname{curl}\mathbf{a} + \operatorname{curl}\mathbf{a}_e.$$

Here, according to the fundamental equations, $-\operatorname{curl}\mathbf{a}$ represents the magnetic current **k**. By analogy, $-\operatorname{curl}\mathbf{a}_e$ can also be said to represent a magnetic current $\mathbf{k}_e$. By this current the intrinsic polarization, say in a turmaline-crystal, can be represented, in the same way as the intrinsic magnetization can be represented, according to AMPERE's theory, by a distribution of electric currents.

Now in the case of a stationary field the current $-\operatorname{curl}\mathbf{a}$ can only exist in material bodies, not in the surrounding ether. And the current $-\operatorname{curl}\mathbf{a}_e$, or the vector $\mathbf{a}_e = 1/\alpha\mathbf{A}_e$ from which it is derived, never exists outside material bodies (10, d).   Therefore, in the case of a stationary field it will be sufficient to apply the second integral in (d) to material bodies only.

From the symmetry of the two sets of equations it is seen at once that the integral expressing the energy of the magnetic field, namely,

$$\Psi = \tfrac{1}{2} \int \mathbf{B} \cdot \mathbf{b}_a d\tau,$$

can be transformed to a form corresponding to (d), namely,

$$\Psi = \tfrac{1}{2} \int \psi \; \text{div} \; \mathbf{B} d\tau + \tfrac{1}{2} \int \mathbf{H} \cdot \text{curl} \; \mathbf{b}_a d\tau,$$

involving thus the true density of magnetism, div $\mathbf{B}$, and the electric current, curl $\mathbf{B}_a$, which is made up of the true electric current, curl $\mathbf{b}$, and the fictitious current, curl $\mathbf{b}_e$, by which, according to AMPERE'S theory, the intrinsic magnetization can be represented.   Now under stationary conditions the true current, curl $\mathbf{a}$, only exists in material bodies, not in the ether, and the quantities div $\mathbf{B}$ and curl $\mathbf{b}_a$ never exist except in material bodies.

We can therefore assert that the energy of the stationary field, whether it be electric or magnetic, can be expressed by integrals which apply to material bodies only, not to the surrounding ether.

15. *Conditions for the Vanishing of the Stationary Field.*—Let us consider now the stationary electric field in the case where there exists no true electrification, div $\mathbf{A} = 0$, no energetic field intensity, $\mathbf{a}_e = 0$, and no true current, curl $\mathbf{a} = 0$.   We shall then have

$$\text{div} \; \mathbf{A} = 0, \qquad \text{curl} \; \mathbf{a}_a = 0,$$

and under these circumstances the energy of the field disappears completely, as is seen from the expression (13, d).   But according to the expression (13, e) for the same energy, which is the sum of only positive elements, the flux $\mathbf{A}$ must disappear in every part of the field.   But when both the flux $\mathbf{A}$ and the energetic field intensity disappear, it is seen from the equations of connection that the induced field intensity will also disappear, and there will exist no electric field at all. In the case of the magnetic field perfectly parallel conclusions can be drawn. Thus:

If there exists no true electrification, no energetic flux, and no magnetic current, there will exist no stationary electric field.

If there exists no true magnetism, no energetic flux, and no electric current, there will exist no stationary magnetic field.

16. *Unique Determinateness of the Stationary Field.*—From this result a new one can be drawn at once. Let us consider two fields, represented by the vectors $\mathbf{A}$, $\mathbf{a}$, and $\mathbf{A'}$, $\mathbf{a'}$, both subject to the condition of having the same distribution of the energetic flux $\mathbf{A}_e$, of the magnetic current $\mathbf{k}$, and of the true electrification E. The equations of the two fields will then be

$$\mathbf{A} = \alpha\mathbf{a} + \mathbf{A}_e, \qquad \mathbf{A'} = \alpha\mathbf{a'} + \mathbf{A}_e,$$
$$\operatorname{curl} \mathbf{a} = -\mathbf{k}, \qquad \operatorname{curl} \mathbf{a'} = -\mathbf{k},$$
$$\operatorname{div} \mathbf{A} = E, \qquad \operatorname{div} \mathbf{A'} = E.$$

Let us consider next the field represented by the difference of the vectors of the two fields, *i. e.*, the field

$$\mathbf{A''} = \mathbf{A'} - \mathbf{A},$$
$$\mathbf{a''} = \mathbf{a'} - \mathbf{a}.$$

As is seen at once, this field will be subject to the conditions

$$\mathbf{A''} = \alpha\mathbf{a''},$$
$$\operatorname{curl} \mathbf{a''} = 0,$$
$$\operatorname{div} \mathbf{A''} = 0.$$

It will thus be a field having no energetic flux, no magnetic current, and no true electrification, and it will disappear completely according to the result above. Thus the fields $\mathbf{A}$, $\mathbf{a}$, and $\mathbf{A'}$, $\mathbf{a'}$, cannot differ from each other.

Perfectly parallel developments can be given for the magnetic field, and we arrive thus at the following parallel results:

According to our system of equations, *the stationary electric field is uniquely determined by the distribution of true electrification, of energetic electric flux, and of magnetic current,* and *the stationary magnetic field is uniquely determined by the distribution of true magnetism, of energetic magnetic flux, and of electric current*

These theorems show the amount of knowledge of the geometry of the stationary fields which is laid down in the equations (11, *b*) They contain in the most condensed form possible our whole knowledge of this geometry   And the importance of these theorems for our purpose is perfectly clear   if we succeed later in representing the hydrodynamic field by a similar system of equations, there will, under similar conditions, be no chance for difference in the geometric properties of the hydrodynamic field, and the stationary electric or magnetic field

But before we proceed to the investigation of the hydrodynamic field we have to consider the dynamic properties of the electric and the magnetic field

10

IV

THE DYNAMIC PROPERTIES OF ELECTROMAG-
NETIC FIELDS ACCORDING TO
MAXWELL'S THEORY.

1. *Electric and Magnetic Energy.* — The MAXWELL equations give, as I have emphasized, only a geometric theory, bearing upon the distribution in space of a series of vectors whose physical meaning is perfectly unknown to us. To give this theory a physical content an additional knowledge is wanted, and this is afforded by our experience relating to the transformations of energy in the electromagnetic field.

The safest way, in our present state of knowledge, of establishing this dynamical theory of the electromagnetic field, seems to be this; start with the expression which is believed to represent the energy of the electric and of the magnetic field, and bring into application the universal principle of the conservation of energy.

The general feature of the method to be used is thus perfectly clear; nevertheless, the details will be open to discussion. First of all, there is no perfect accordance between the different writers with regard to the true expression of the energy of the fields. All authors agree that it is a volume integral in which the function to be integrated is the half scalar product of a flux and a field intensity. But opinions seem to differ as to whether it should be the actual fluxes and field intensities or only the induced ones. Following HEAVISIDE, I suppose that the *actual* fluxes and field intensities are the proper vectors for expressing the energy, and thus write the expression for the total energy of the electromagnetic field

$$\Phi + \Psi = \int \tfrac{1}{2}\mathbf{A} \cdot \mathbf{a}_a d\tau + \int \tfrac{1}{2}\mathbf{B} \cdot \mathbf{b}_a d\tau.$$

Here, the first integral gives the amount of the electric, and the second the amount of the magnetic energy, the integrations being extended over the whole field

2   *Localization and Continuity of Energy* — Starting with this expression for the energy of the field and bringing into application the principle of the conservation of energy, we can of course deduce only results strictly in accordance with the experience which led us to this form of expression for the energy   We are able then to derive the amount of mechanical work done, and consequently the forces doing it, for the case when the different bodies in the field are displaced relatively to each other

But for the sake of the problem before us, it is very desirable to go a step further, to determine not only the resultant forces acting against the bodies as a whole, but also the system of elementary forces, which act upon the elements of volume of the bodies, and of which the resultant forces are composed   Of these elementary forces we have only a very limited experimental knowledge, and to derive them, additional knowledge is needed, which is not contained in the mere statements of the form of the energy integral and of the principle of the conservation of energy We do not possess this in universally accepted form, but we admit as working hypotheses the following two principles

First, we suppose that it is allowable to speak not only of *amounts* of energy, but also of a *distribution of energy* in space That this should be so is, *a priori*, not at all clear   The universal principle of the conservation of energy relates only to amounts of energy   And in the model science relating to energy, abstract dynamics, the notion of a certain distribution of energy in space seems to be often of rather questionable clearness and utility   But still it may have a more or less limited usefulness   Assuming this, we admit as a working hypothesis, that the energy integral not only gives the total amount of electric and magnetic energy, but also the distribution of this energy in space, the amount of energy per unit volume in the field being

$$\tfrac{1}{2}A\ a_a + \tfrac{1}{2}B\ b_a$$

To this principle of the *localization of energy* we add the second, the principle of the *continuity of energy*, which is this: energy cannot enter a space without passing through the surface surrounding this space. This principle forces us to admit a more or less determined *motion of the energy*, which in connection with the transformations of the energy regulates the distribution of the electromagnetic energy in space. To this principle we may make similar objections as to the previous one. The idea of a determinate motion of the energy does not in abstract dynamics seem to be always very clear or useful, even though it may seem to have in this branch of physics also a certain limited meaning. And even though considerable doubt may fall upon these two suppositions considered as universal principles, no deciding argument can be given at present *against* their use to a limited extent as working hypotheses.

3. *Electric and Magnetic Activity.* — To these abstract and general principles we have to add definite suppositions suggested more or less by experiment. The first is this: the rate at which the electric or magnetic energy is created by the foreign sources of energy is given per unit volume by the scalar product of the energetic field intensity into the corresponding current. This principle was originally suggested by the observation that the rate of doing work by the voltaic battery was the product of its intrinsic electromotive force and the current produced by it. And it is generalized by inductive reasoning so that it is made to include every impressed or energetic force and field intensity, every current, electric or magnetic, conduction current, or displacement current.

Starting thus with MAXWELL's equations for the general case of a moving medium

$$c = \text{curl } b,$$

$$k = - \text{curl } a,$$

we can at once find the rate at which energy is supplied per unit volume by the foreign sources of energy. For, multiplying these equations by the energetic field intensities and adding, we get

(a) $\quad$ $a_e\,c + b_e\,k = a_e\,\text{curl }b - b_e\,\text{curl }a$

The left hand member gives the rate at which this energy is supplied. The discussion of the right hand member therefore will show how the energy supplied is stored, transformed, or moved to other places. In this discussion we shall follow the method indicated by HEAVISIDE *

4 *Storage, Transformation, and Motion of the Energy* — To examine the right hand member of the equation we express the energetic field intensities as the differences of the actual and the induced field intensities,

$$a_e = a_a - a, \qquad b_e = b_a - b$$

The equation of activity then takes the form

(a) $a_e\,c + b_e\,k = a_a\,\text{curl }b - b_a\,\text{curl }a - a\,\text{curl }b + b\,\text{curl }a$

For the last two forms we write, according to a well known vector formula,

(b) $\quad$ $-a\,\text{curl }b + b\,\text{curl }a = \text{div}(a \times b)$

In the first term on the right hand side of equation (a) we introduce for curl b the developed expression for the electric current, (III, 10, b_2) Thus

(c) $a_a\,\text{curl }b = a_a\,\dfrac{\partial A}{\partial t} + a_a'\,\text{curl}(A \times V) + a_a\,V\,\text{div }A + \dfrac{1}{T}\,a_a\,A$

Remembering that $A = \alpha a_a$, we find easily,

$$a_a\,\frac{\partial A}{\partial t} = a_a\,\frac{\partial(\alpha a_a)}{\partial t} = \alpha a_a\,\frac{\partial a_a}{\partial t} + a_a^2\,\frac{\partial \alpha}{\partial t}$$

$$= \tfrac{1}{2}\alpha\,\frac{\partial a_a^2}{\partial t} + a_a^2\,\frac{\partial \alpha}{\partial t}$$

$$= \frac{\partial}{\partial t}(\tfrac{1}{2}\alpha a_a^2) - \tfrac{1}{2}a_a^2\,\frac{\partial \alpha}{\partial t} + a_a^2\,\frac{\partial \alpha}{\partial t}$$

or finally

*O HEAVISIDE On the forces, stresses and fluxes of energy in the electromagnetic field Transactions of the Royal Society, London, 1892 Electrical papers, Vol II, p. 521

$$\mathbf{a}_a \cdot \frac{\partial \mathbf{A}}{\partial t} = \frac{\partial}{\partial t}\left(\tfrac{1}{2}\mathbf{A}\cdot\mathbf{a}_a\right) + \tfrac{1}{2}a_a^2\frac{\partial\alpha}{\partial t}$$

Now we have in general (III., 10, b_3)

$$\frac{\partial\alpha}{\partial t} = \frac{d\alpha}{dt} - \mathbf{V}\cdot\bigtriangledown\alpha.$$

And if we suppose that the moving individual element does not change the value of its inductivity as a consequence of the motion, we have $d\alpha/dt = 0$, and

$$\frac{\partial\alpha}{\partial t} = -\mathbf{V}\cdot\bigtriangledown\alpha.$$

And therefore

(c_1) $\qquad\qquad \mathbf{a}_a \cdot \dfrac{\partial \mathbf{A}}{\partial t} = \dfrac{\partial}{\partial t}\left(\tfrac{1}{2}\mathbf{A}\cdot\mathbf{a}_a\right) - \mathbf{V}\cdot\tfrac{1}{2}a_a^2\bigtriangledown\alpha.$

Passing to the next term in (c), we can transform it by the vector formula (b), writing $\mathbf{a}_a$ for $\mathbf{a}$ and $\mathbf{A}\times\mathbf{V}$ for $\mathbf{b}$.   Thus

$$\mathbf{a}_a\cdot\operatorname{curl}(\mathbf{A}\times\mathbf{V}) = \mathbf{A}\times\mathbf{V}\cdot\operatorname{curl}\mathbf{a}_a - \operatorname{div}\left[\mathbf{a}_a\times(\mathbf{A}\times\mathbf{V})\right].$$

In the first right hand term we interchange cross and dot, and change the order of factors by cyclic permutation.   In the second term we develope the triple vector product according to the well-known formula; we have then

(c_2) $\mathbf{a}_a\cdot\operatorname{curl}(\mathbf{A}\times\mathbf{V}) = \mathbf{V}\cdot(\operatorname{curl}\mathbf{a}_a)\times\mathbf{A} + \operatorname{div}\left[(\mathbf{a}_a\cdot\mathbf{A})\mathbf{V} - (\mathbf{a}_a\cdot\mathbf{V})\mathbf{A}\right].$

Substituting (c_1) and (c_2) in (c) we get

(d) $\qquad \mathbf{a}_a\cdot\operatorname{curl}\mathbf{b} = \dfrac{\partial}{\partial t}\left(\tfrac{1}{2}\mathbf{A}\cdot\mathbf{a}_a\right) + \dfrac{1}{T}\mathbf{A}\cdot\mathbf{a}_a + \mathbf{V}\cdot\{(\operatorname{div}\mathbf{A})\mathbf{a}_a$

$\qquad\qquad - \tfrac{1}{2}a_a^2\bigtriangledown\alpha + (\operatorname{curl}\mathbf{a}_a)\times\mathbf{A}\} + \operatorname{div}\{(\mathbf{A}\cdot\mathbf{a}_a)\mathbf{V} - (\mathbf{a}_a\cdot\mathbf{V})\mathbf{A}\}.$

In exactly the same way, introducing the full expression for the magnetic current, we have

(e) $\qquad -\mathbf{b}_a\cdot\operatorname{curl}\mathbf{a} = \dfrac{\partial}{\partial t}\left(\tfrac{1}{2}\mathbf{B}\cdot\mathbf{b}_a\right) + \dfrac{1}{T}\mathbf{B}\cdot\mathbf{b}_a + \mathbf{V}\{(\operatorname{div}\mathbf{B})\mathbf{b}_a$

$\qquad\qquad - \tfrac{1}{2}b_a^2\bigtriangledown\beta + (\operatorname{curl}\mathbf{b}_a)\times\mathbf{B}\} + \operatorname{div}\{(\mathbf{B}\cdot\mathbf{b}_a)\mathbf{V} - (\mathbf{b}_a\cdot\mathbf{V})\mathbf{B}\}.$

The developments (b), (d), and (e) are now introduced in (a). Suitably distributing the terms, we get

$$a_s \, c + b_s \, k = \frac{\partial}{\partial t} \{ \tfrac{1}{2} A \; a_a + \tfrac{1}{2} B \; b_a \}$$

$$+ \frac{1}{T} A \; a_a + \frac{1}{T'} B \; b_a$$

$$(f) \qquad + V \; \{ (\text{div } A) a_a - \tfrac{1}{2} a_a^2 \nabla \alpha + (\text{curl } a_a) \times A \}$$

$$+ V \; \{ (\text{div } B) b_a - \tfrac{1}{2} b_a^2 \nabla \beta + (\text{curl } b_a) \times B \}$$

$$+ \text{div} \{ a \times b + \tfrac{1}{2} (A \; a_a + B \; b_a) V \}$$

$$+ \text{div} \{ -(a_a \; V) A + \tfrac{1}{2} (A \; a_a) V - (b_a \; V) B + \tfrac{1}{2} (B \; b_a) V \},$$

which is the completely developed form of the equation of activity. The first member gives, as we have said, the rate of supply of electromagnetic energy per unit volume, and the second member shows how the energy supplied is used. Taking one term after the other in each line, the common interpretation of them is this. The first term

$$\frac{\partial}{\partial t} \{ \tfrac{1}{2} A \; a_a + \tfrac{1}{2} B \; b_a \}$$

gives the part of the energy supplied which is simply stored as electric and magnetic energy in the unit volume. The second term

$$\frac{1}{T} A \; a_a + \frac{1}{T'} B \; b_a$$

gives the part of the energy supplied which is wasted as heat, according to JOULE's law, the waste due to the fictitious magnetic conduction current being also formally included.

The following two terms contain the velocity **V** of the moving material element of volume as a scalar factor. As the equation is an equation of activity, the other factor must necessarily be a force, in the common dynamic sense of this word, referred to unit volume of the moving particle. These factors are then the forces exerted by the electromagnetic system against the exterior forces, the factor of the first term being the mechanical force depending on the electric field, and the factor of the second term being the force depending upon the magnetic field,

$$(g) \quad \begin{aligned} \mathbf{f}_e &= (\text{div } \mathbf{A})\mathbf{a}_a - \tfrac{1}{2}\mathbf{a}_a^2 \nabla \alpha + (\text{curl } \mathbf{a}_a) \times \mathbf{A}, \\ \mathbf{f}_m &= (\text{div } \mathbf{B})\mathbf{b}_a - \tfrac{1}{2}\mathbf{b}_a^2 \nabla \beta + (\text{curl } \mathbf{b}_a) \times \mathbf{B}. \end{aligned}$$

The first of the two terms of (f) which have the form of a divergence gives, according to the common interpretation, that part of the energy supplied which moves away. There are two reasons for this motion of energy, first, the radiation of energy, given by the Poynting-flux

$$\mathbf{a} \times \mathbf{b},$$

and second, the pure convection of electromagnetic energy, given by the vector

$$\tfrac{1}{2}(\mathbf{A} \cdot \mathbf{a}_a + \mathbf{B} \cdot \mathbf{b}_a)\mathbf{V},$$

which is simply the product of the energy per unit volume into the velocity.

Finally, the last term gives, according to the common interpretation, that part of the energy supplied which, in terms of the theory of the motion of energy, moves away in consequence of the stress in the medium which is the seat of the field, the flux of energy depending upon this stress being given by the vector

$$- (\mathbf{a}_a \cdot \mathbf{V})\mathbf{A} + \tfrac{1}{2}(\mathbf{A} \cdot \mathbf{a}_a)\mathbf{V} - (\mathbf{b}_a \cdot \mathbf{V})\mathbf{B} + \tfrac{1}{2}(\mathbf{B} \cdot \mathbf{b}_a)\mathbf{V},$$

whose divergence appears in the equation of activity. For this flux of energy may be considered as that due to a stress, the component of which against a plane whose orientation is given by the unit normal $\mathbf{N}$ is

$$\mathbf{a}_a(\mathbf{A} \cdot \mathbf{N}) - (\tfrac{1}{2}\mathbf{A} \cdot \mathbf{a}_a)\mathbf{N} + \mathbf{b}_a(\mathbf{B} \cdot \mathbf{N}) - (\tfrac{1}{2}\mathbf{B} \cdot \mathbf{b}_a)\mathbf{N}.$$

This stress splits up into an electric and a magnetic stress. And, in the case of isotropy, which we assume, the first of these stresses consists of a tension parallel to, and a pressure perpendicular to the lines of electric force, in amount equal to the electric energy per unit volume ; the second consists of a tension and pressure bearing the same relation to the magnetic lines of force and magnetic energy per unit volume.   This is seen when the unit normal **N** is drawn first parallel to, and then normal to the corresponding lines of force.

The theory thus developed may be given with somewhat greater generality and with greater care in the details.   Thus the anisotropy of the medium, already existing, or produced as a consequence of the motion, can be fully taken into account, as well as the changes produced by the motion in the values of the inductivities and in the values of the energetic vectors.   On the other hand, there exist differences of opinion with regard to the details of the theory.   But setting these aside and considering the question from the point of view of principles, is the theory safely founded ?   If we knew the real physical significance of the electric and magnetic vectors, should we then in the developements above meet no contradictions?

This question may be difficult to answer.   The theory must necessarily contain a core of truth.   The results which we can derive from it, and which depend solely upon the principle of the *conservation* of energy and upon the expression of the electromagnetic energy, so far as this expression is empirically tested, must of course be true.   But for the rest of the theory we can only say, that it is the best theory of the dynamic properties of the electromagnetic field that we possess.

5. *The Forces in the Electromagnetic Field.*—What particularly interests us is the expression for the mechanical forces in the field, (4, *g*).   As the expressions for the electric and the magnetic force have exactly the same form, it will be sufficient to consider one of them.   Let us take the magnetic force,

$$\mathbf{f} = (\text{div } \mathbf{B})\mathbf{b}_a - \tfrac{1}{2}\mathbf{b}_a^2 \nabla\beta + (\text{curl } \mathbf{b}_a) \times \mathbf{B}.$$

This is a force per unit volume, and if our theory is correct, this expression should give the true distribution of the force acting upon

11

the elements of volume, and not merely the true value of the resultant force upon the whole body. The significance of each term is obvious. The first term gives the force upon the true magnetism, if this exists. It has the direction of the actual field intensity, and is equal to this vector multiplied by the magnetism. The second term depends upon the heterogeneity of the bodies, and gives, therefore, the force depending upon the induced magnetism. The elementary force which underlies the resultant forces observed in the experiments of induced magnetism should therefore be a force which has the direction of the gradient, $-\nabla\beta$, of the inductivity β, and which is equal in amount to the product of this gradient into the magnetic energy per unit volume. When we consider a body as a whole, the gradient of energy will exist principally in the layer between the body and the surrounding medium. It will point outwards if the body has greater inductivity than the medium, but its average value for the whole body will be nil in every direction. But the force, which is the product of this vector into half the square of the field intensity, will therefore have greater average values at the places of great absolute field intensity, quite irrespective of its direction. Hence, the body will move in the direction which the inductivity gradient has at the places of the greatest absolute strength of the field, i. e., the body will move in the direction of increasing absolute strength of the field. And, in the same way, it is seen that a body which has smaller inductivity than the surrounding field will move in the direction of decreasing absolute strength of the field. The expression thus contains FARADAY's well known qualitative law for the motion of magnetic or diamagnetic bodies in the magnetic field.

The third term of the equation contains two distinct forces, which, having the same form, are combined into one. Splitting the actual field intensity into its induced and energetic parts and treating the curl of the vector in the same way, we get

$$\operatorname{curl} \mathbf{b}_a = \operatorname{curl} \mathbf{b} + \operatorname{curl} \mathbf{b}_e = \mathbf{c} + \mathbf{c}_e,$$

where $\mathbf{c}$ is *the true* electric current, and $\mathbf{c}_e$ the fictitious current, by which, according to AMPERE's theory, the permanent magnetism may be represented. The last term of the expression for the force therefore splits into two,

$$(\text{curl } \mathbf{b}_a) \times \mathbf{B} = \mathbf{c} \times \mathbf{B} + \mathbf{c}_s \times \mathbf{B},$$

where the first term is the well known expression for the force per unit volume in a body carrying an electric current of density c. The second term gives the force upon permanent magnetization, and according to the theory developed, this force should be the same as the force upon the equivalent distribution of electric current.

6. *The Resultant Force.* — As we have remarked, our developments may possibly contain errors which we cannot detect in the present state of our knowledge. The value found for the elementary forces may be wrong. But however this may be, we know *this* with perfect certainty; if we integrate the elementary forces for the whole volume of a body, we shall arrive at *the true value of the resultant force* to which the body as a whole is subject. For calculating this resultant force, we come back to the results of the observations which form the empirical foundation of our knowledge of the dynamic properties of the electromagnetic field. A perfectly safe result of our theory will therefore consist in the fact that the expression

$$(a) \quad \mathbf{F} = \int (\text{div } \mathbf{B}) \mathbf{b}_a d\tau - \int \tfrac{1}{2} \mathbf{b}_a^2 \nabla \beta d\tau + \int (\text{curl } \mathbf{b}_a) \times \mathbf{B} d\tau,$$

where the integration is extended over a whole body, gives the true value of the resultant force upon the body. By a whole body, we understand any body surrounded by a perfectly homogeneous gaseous or fluid dielectric of the constant inductivity β_0, which is itself not the seat of any magnetism M, of any energetic magnetic flux $\mathbf{B}_s$, or of any electric current c. To avoid mathematical prolixity we suppose that the properties of the body change continuously into those of the ether, the layer in which these changes take place being always considered as belonging to the body. Thus at its surface the body has all the properties of the ether. By this supposition, we shall avoid the introduction of surface integrals, which usually appear when transformations of volume integrals are made.

By transformations of the integrals we can pass from the above expression for the resultant force to a series of equivalent expressions. To find one of these new expressions we split the actual field intensity into its two parts,

$$\mathbf{b}_a = \mathbf{b} + \mathbf{b}_e,$$

and we get

(b) $\mathbf{F} = \int (\operatorname{div} \mathbf{B})\mathbf{b} d\tau - \int \tfrac{1}{2}\mathbf{b}^2 \triangledown \beta d\tau + \int (\operatorname{curl} \mathbf{b}) \times \cdot \mathbf{B} d\tau + \mathbf{J},$$

where

(b')
$$\mathbf{J} = \int (\operatorname{div} \mathbf{B})\mathbf{b}_e d\tau - \int (\mathbf{b} \cdot \mathbf{b}_e) \triangledown \beta d\tau$$
$$- \int \tfrac{1}{2}\mathbf{b}_e^2 \triangledown \beta d\tau + \int (\operatorname{curl} \mathbf{b}_e) \times \mathbf{B} d\tau.$$

To reduce the expression for $\mathbf{J}$ we consider the first term. Transforming according to well known formulæ, we get

$$\int (\operatorname{div} \mathbf{B})\mathbf{b}_e d\tau = - \int \mathbf{B} \triangledown \mathbf{b}_e d\tau = - \int \mathbf{B}\mathbf{b}_e \triangledown d\tau - \int (\operatorname{curl} \mathbf{b}_e) \times \mathbf{B} d\tau.$$

Substituting, we get $\mathbf{J}$ reduced to three terms,

(b'') $\mathbf{J} = - \int \mathbf{B}\mathbf{b}_e \triangledown d\tau - \int (\mathbf{b} \cdot \mathbf{b}_e) \triangledown \beta d\tau - \int \tfrac{1}{2}\mathbf{b}_e^2 \triangledown \beta d\tau.$

Introducing in the first of these integrals $\mathbf{B} = \beta\mathbf{b} + \beta\mathbf{b}_e$, we get

$$- \int \mathbf{B}\mathbf{b}_e \triangledown d\tau = - \int \beta (\mathbf{b}\mathbf{b}_e \triangledown) d\tau - \int \beta (\mathbf{b}_e \mathbf{b}_e \triangledown) d\tau,$$

in which we have to remember that the operator $\triangledown$ works only upon the vector immediately preceding it. In the first of the two integrals of the right hand member we join the scalar factor β with the vector $\mathbf{b}_e$ upon which $\triangledown$ works, remembering $\beta\mathbf{b}_e = \mathbf{B}_e$. A term containing $\triangledown\beta$ must then be subtracted. The second integral we can change, letting the operator $\triangledown$ work upon both factors. Then

$$- \int \mathbf{B}\mathbf{b}_e \triangledown d\tau = - \int \mathbf{b}\mathbf{B}_e \triangledown d\tau + \int (\mathbf{b} \cdot \mathbf{b}_e) \triangledown \beta d\tau - \int \tfrac{1}{2}\beta \triangledown \mathbf{b}_e^2 d\tau.$$

Finally, integrating the last term by parts and remembering that b_e disappears at the surface of the body,

$$- \int \mathbf{B} b_e \bigtriangledown d\tau = - \int \mathbf{b} \mathbf{B}_e \bigtriangledown d\tau + \int (\mathbf{b} \cdot \mathbf{b}_e) \bigtriangledown \beta d\tau + \int \tfrac{1}{2} \mathbf{b}_e^2 \bigtriangledown \beta d\tau.$$

Substituting this in (b''), we get simply

(b''') $$\qquad\qquad\qquad\qquad \mathbf{J} = - \int \mathbf{b} \mathbf{B}_e \bigtriangledown d\tau.$$

This leads to the expression

(c) $$\mathbf{F} = \int (\mathrm{div}\ \mathbf{B}) \mathbf{b} d\tau - \int \tfrac{1}{2} \mathbf{b}^2 \bigtriangledown \beta d\tau + \int (\mathrm{curl}\ \mathbf{b}) \times \mathbf{B} d\tau - \int \mathbf{b} \mathbf{B}_e \bigtriangledown d\tau$$

for the resultant force. The four terms give the forces depending upon the true magnetism, the induced magnetism, the electric current distribution, and the permanent magnetization respectively. The resultant force is represented here by a system of elementary forces, given by

$$\mathbf{f}_2 = (\mathrm{div}\ \mathbf{B}) \mathbf{b} - \tfrac{1}{2} \mathbf{b}^2 \bigtriangledown \mathbf{B} - \mathbf{b} \mathbf{B}_e \bigtriangledown + (\mathrm{curl}\ \mathbf{b}) \times \mathbf{B}.$$

These elementary forces must be considered as fictitious if the expression found above represents the true values of the elementary forces. But if our developments have not been altogether trustworthy, the reverse might also be the case, or else none of them may give the true values of the elementary forces, while both of them give the true values of the resultant forces.

7. *Other Forms for the Resultant Force.* — In writing the expression for the resultant force we have hitherto used scalars and vectors of a fundamental nature. By the introduction of certain auxiliary scalars or vectors the expression for the resultant force may be brought to forms of remarkable simplicity. But as this is obtained at the cost of the introduction of artificial quantities, the possibility that the expressions under the integral signs represent the real elementary forces is lost.

The transformation to these simple forms of the expression for the resultant force depends upon the introduction of a vector $\mathbf{B}_f$ defined by the equation

(a) $$\qquad\qquad\qquad\qquad \mathbf{B} = \beta_0 \mathbf{b} + \mathbf{B}_f.$$

This has the form of the true equation of connection, except that the constant inductivity β_0 of the ether is introduced instead of the true inductivity of the body. $\mathbf{B}_f$ is therefore a virtual energetic flux, to compensate for our leaving out of consideration the variations of the inductivity. This is the well known artifice of POISSON's theory of induced magnetism, which enables us to treat the induced magnetism as if it were permanent.

To introduce this vector into the expression for the resultant force we first remark that in the second integral of the expression (6, c) we can write $\beta - \beta_0$ instead of β. Performing the integration by parts throughout the whole volume of the body and remembering that $\beta - \beta_0$ disappears at the surface of the body, we get

$$- \int \tfrac{1}{2} \mathbf{b}^2 \triangledown \beta d\tau = - \int \tfrac{1}{2} \mathbf{b}^2 \triangledown (\beta - \beta_0) d\tau$$

$$= \int \tfrac{1}{2} (\beta - \beta_0) \triangledown \mathbf{b}^2 d\tau$$

$$= \int (\beta - \beta_0) \mathbf{b} \mathbf{b} \triangledown d\tau.$$

In like manner, the transformation by parts of the integral in the expression (6, c) expressing the force upon permanent magnetism gives

$$- \int \mathbf{b} \mathbf{B}_e \triangledown d\tau = \int \mathbf{B}_e \mathbf{b} \triangledown d\tau.$$

The integrals for the temporary and the permanent force may now be added, and remarking that equation (a), in connection with the fundamental equation of connection, gives $\mathbf{B}_f = (\beta - \beta_0)\mathbf{b} + \mathbf{B}_e$, we get

$$- \int \tfrac{1}{2} \mathbf{b}^2 \triangledown \beta d\tau - \int \mathbf{b} \mathbf{B}_e \triangledown d\tau = \int \mathbf{B}_f \mathbf{b} \triangledown d\tau.$$

The substitution of this in (6, c) gives the following more compact form of the expression for the resultant force

(b) $\qquad \mathbf{F} = \int (\mathrm{div}\ \mathbf{B}) \mathbf{b} d\tau + \int \mathbf{B}_f \mathbf{b} \triangledown d\tau + \int (\mathrm{curl}\ \mathbf{b}) \times \mathbf{B} d\tau.$

Here, the resultant force seems to come from an elementary force

$$\mathbf{f}_3 = (\mathrm{div}\ \mathbf{B}) \mathbf{b} + \mathbf{B}_f \mathbf{b} \triangledown + (\mathrm{curl}\ \mathbf{b}) \times \mathbf{B}.$$

A still shorter form of the resultant force and of the corresponding fictitious elementary force may be found as follows. According to a well known vector formula, we can write

$$\int \mathbf{B}_f \mathbf{b} \triangledown d\tau = \int \mathbf{B}_f \triangledown \mathbf{b} d\tau - \int (\text{curl } \mathbf{b}) \times \mathbf{B}_f d\tau.$$

Transforming the first integral of the second member according to a well known formula and remembering that $\mathbf{B}_f = 0$ at the surface of the body, we get

$$\int \mathbf{B}_f \mathbf{b} \triangledown d\tau = - \int (\text{div } \mathbf{B}_f) \mathbf{b} d\tau - \int (\text{curl } \mathbf{b}) \times \mathbf{B}_f d\tau.$$

Introducing this expression and remarking that, according to (a), div $\mathbf{B} = \beta_0$ div $\mathbf{b}$ + div $\mathbf{B}_f$, we get

$$\mathbf{F} = \beta_0 \int (\text{div } \mathbf{b}) \mathbf{b} d\tau + \beta_0 \int (\text{curl } \mathbf{b}) \times \mathbf{b} d\tau,$$

which is the most concise form of the expression for the resultant force. It is expressed here by a fictitious elementary force

$$\mathbf{f}_4 = \beta_0 (\text{div } \mathbf{b}) \mathbf{b} + \beta_0 (\text{curl } \mathbf{b}) \times \mathbf{b}.$$

The divergence of the field intensity, which appears here, is called the free density of magnetism. The force upon true magnetism, upon permanent magnetic polarization, and upon induced magnetism can be condensed into one expression, and the whole force is expressed in an exceedingly simple way by the field intensity, its divergence, its curl, and the inductivity of the surrounding medium.

8. *Resumé* — It will be convenient on account of the following lectures to sum up the fundamental equations for the stationary electric, and the stationary magnetic field. Using for the description of the fields the vectors of scheme III., and in some cases even the artificial vectors $\mathbf{A}_f$ or $\mathbf{B}_f$ (IV., 7, a), we have first a set of equations of connection, by use of which we introduce in the fundamental equations the vector wanted for any special purpose. Of these equations of connection we note the following, referring for more special cases to the complete system (III., 7, a).

$$\text{(A)} \quad \begin{array}{ll} \textit{Electric} & \textit{Magnetic} \\[4pt] \mathbf{A} = \alpha\mathbf{a}_a, & \mathbf{B} = \beta\mathbf{b}_a, \\[4pt] \quad = \alpha\mathbf{a} + \mathbf{A}_e, & \quad = \beta\mathbf{b} + \mathbf{B}_e, \\[4pt] \quad = \alpha_0\mathbf{a} + \mathbf{A}_f, & \quad = \beta_0\mathbf{b} + \mathbf{B}_f. \end{array}$$

Then we have the proper equations of the fields, which express the relation between the field intensity and the current density,

$$\text{(B)} \qquad\qquad \operatorname{curl} \mathbf{a} = -\mathbf{k}, \qquad \operatorname{curl} \mathbf{b} = \mathbf{c}.$$

Finally, we have the equations of definition for the density of electrification, or of magnetism,

$$\text{(C)} \qquad\qquad \operatorname{div} \mathbf{A} = E, \qquad \operatorname{div} \mathbf{B} = M.$$

To complete the geometric description of the field we have finally a number of special conditions which are fulfilled in the free ether, namely,

$$\text{(D}_1) \qquad\qquad \alpha = \alpha_0, \qquad \beta = \beta_0,$$

$$\text{(D}_2) \qquad\qquad E = 0, \qquad M = 0,$$

$$\text{(D}_3) \qquad\qquad \mathbf{k} = 0, \qquad \mathbf{c} = 0,$$

$$\text{(D}_4) \qquad\qquad \mathbf{A}_e = 0, \qquad \mathbf{B}_e = 0.$$

This set of equations gives, in the sense of the theorems (III., 16), a complete description of the geometry of the fields.

Our knowledge of the dynamics of the field is less complete. According to the analysis of HEAVISIDE, we have reason to believe that the elementary force in the field per unit volume is given by the expression

$$\text{(E}_1) \quad \begin{aligned} \mathbf{f}_{e,1} &= (\operatorname{div} \mathbf{A})\mathbf{a}_a - \tfrac{1}{2}\mathbf{a}_a^2 \nabla\alpha + (\operatorname{curl} \mathbf{a}_a) \times \mathbf{A}, \\[4pt] \mathbf{f}_{m,1} &= (\operatorname{div} \mathbf{B})\mathbf{b}_a - \tfrac{1}{2}\mathbf{b}_a^2 \nabla\beta + (\operatorname{curl} \mathbf{b}_a) \times \mathbf{B}. \end{aligned}$$

But other forms are not excluded, and we may have

$$\text{(E}_2) \quad \begin{aligned} \mathbf{f}_{e,2} &= (\operatorname{div} \mathbf{A})\mathbf{a} - \tfrac{1}{2}\mathbf{a}^2 \nabla\alpha + (\operatorname{curl} \mathbf{a}) \times \mathbf{A} - \mathbf{a}\mathbf{A}_e \nabla, \\[4pt] \mathbf{f}_{m,2} &= (\operatorname{div} \mathbf{B})\mathbf{b} - \tfrac{1}{2}\mathbf{b}^2 \nabla\beta + (\operatorname{curl} \mathbf{b}) \times \mathbf{B} - \mathbf{b}\mathbf{B}_e \nabla. \end{aligned}$$

Our reliable knowledge is reduced to this — we get on integrating any of these forces for a whole body the resultant force which produces the motion of the whole body. The same value of the resultant force may also be found from other purely artificial distributions of the elementary force, for example,

$$(E_3) \qquad \begin{aligned} \mathbf{f}_{e,3} &= (\operatorname{div} \mathbf{A})\mathbf{a} + \mathbf{A}_{,}\mathbf{a}\triangledown + (\operatorname{curl} \mathbf{a}) \times \mathbf{A}, \\ \mathbf{f}_{m,3} &= (\operatorname{div} \mathbf{B})\mathbf{b} + \mathbf{B}_{,}\mathbf{b}\triangledown + (\operatorname{curl} \mathbf{b}) \times \mathbf{B}, \end{aligned}$$

or

$$(E_4) \qquad \begin{aligned} \mathbf{f}_{e,4} &= \alpha_0(\operatorname{div} \mathbf{a})\mathbf{a} + \alpha_0(\operatorname{curl} \mathbf{a}) \times \mathbf{a}, \\ \mathbf{f}_{m,4} &= \beta_0(\operatorname{div} \mathbf{b})\mathbf{b} + \beta_0(\operatorname{curl} \mathbf{b}) \times \mathbf{b}. \end{aligned}$$

12

V.

GEOMETRIC AND DYNAMIC PROPERTIES OF THE HYDRODYNAMIC FIELD. GENERAL DEMONSTRATION OF THE ANALOGY TO THE STATIONARY ELECTRO-MAGNETIC FIELDS.

1. *Preliminary Remarks.* — Our preliminary investigations, based on elementary reasoning and experiment, have already given the general feature of the analogy, which we are now going to examine more closely. According to these preliminary results, we have no reason to look for an analogy extending beyond the phenomena termed stationary. The main feature of the analogy is given by the correspondence :

flux .... velocity,
field intensity .... specific momentum,
inductivity .... mobility (specific volume).

To facilitate the comparison of the fields I shall denote the hydrodynamic quantities by the same letters as the corresponding electrical quantities. The symmetry in the properties of the electric and magnetic fields will make it possible to pass at once from the comparison with the electric field to the comparison with the magnetic field.

2. *The Hydrodynamic Equations.* — The basis of our investigation will be the hydrodynamic equations, of which there are two; the scalar equation for the conservation of the mass, generally called the equation of continuity, and the vector equation of motion.

α being the specific volume of the fluid, **A** the vector velocity, and d/dt representing the individual time-differentiation, the equation of continuity may be written

$$(a) \qquad \frac{1}{\alpha}\frac{d\alpha}{dt} = \operatorname{div} \mathbf{A}.$$

The first member is the velocity of expansion per unit volume of the moving fluid particle, expressed through the effect of this expansion upon the specific volume, or the volume of unit mass. The second member is the same velocity of expansion expressed through the distribution of velocity in the fluid. The equality of these two expressions of the same velocity of expansion insures the conservation of the mass during the motion of the fluid.

Now $\mathbf{f}$ being the exterior force acting per unit volume of the moving fluid masses, and p the pressure in the fluid, the vector equation of motion may be written

$$(b) \qquad \frac{1}{\alpha}\frac{d\mathbf{A}}{dt} = \mathbf{f} - \nabla p.$$

The first member is the product of the density, $1/\alpha$, of the moving particle into its acceleration, $d\mathbf{A}/dt$, and the second member gives the vector sum of the forces per unit volume acting upon it. These forces are the exterior force $\mathbf{f}$, and the force due to the pressure, $-\nabla p$, generally called the gradient.

In the use of these equations it is always to be remembered that the individual differentiating symbol d/dt is related to the local differentiating symbol $\partial/\partial t$ by the EULERIAN expansion

$$(c) \qquad \frac{d}{dt} = \frac{\partial}{\partial t} + \mathbf{A}\nabla.$$

These equations do not give the geometry and the dynamics of the hydrodynamic field as separate theories. They contain the properties of the fields viewed from one central point, from which their geometric and dynamic properties seem perfectly united. It will be our problem to artificially separate from one another certain geometric and certain dynamic properties, in order to be able to carry out the comparison with those other fields which we know only as the result of an inspection from without, an inspection which has allowed us only to recognize two separate sides of their properties, without any deeper insight into their true relations.

3. *Equation of Continuity — Equation for the Density of Electrification.* — The equation of continuity has the form of one of the fundamental equations of the electric field. To show this we have only to represent the velocity of expansion per unit volume, $1/\alpha \, d\alpha/dt$, by a single letter E, and obtain the equation corresponding to (IV., 8, C),

$$\operatorname{div} \mathbf{A} = E,$$

which, in the interpretation of the symbols for the electrical case, is the equation which gives the density of electrification in the electric field.

4. *Transformation of the Dynamic Equation.* — The dynamic equation does not in its original form show any resemblance to any of the equations of the electric field. Some simple transformations will, however, bring out terms of the same form as appear in the dynamic equations of the electric field.

To show this let us first introduce instead of the velocity $\mathbf{A}$ the actual specific momentum, $\mathbf{a}_a$, according to the equation

(a) $\mathbf{A} = \alpha \mathbf{a}_a.$

The equation of motion then takes the form

$$\frac{d\mathbf{a}_a}{dt} + \frac{1}{\alpha} \frac{d\alpha}{dt} \mathbf{a}_a = \mathbf{f} - \nabla p,$$

or, according to the equation of continuity $(2, a)$,

$$\frac{d\mathbf{a}_a}{dt} + (\operatorname{div} \mathbf{A}) \mathbf{a}_a = \mathbf{f} - \nabla p.$$

In the left hand member we have the term $(\operatorname{div} \mathbf{A})\mathbf{a}_a$, the analogue of which appears in the expression $\mathbf{f}_1$ for the elementary forces in the electric field (IV., 8, E_1). It is the elementary force acting upon the true electrification, $\operatorname{div} \mathbf{A}$.

Further simple transformations bring in the other corresponding terms appearing in the expression for $\mathbf{f}_1$ for the elementary forces in the electric field. Using the Eulerian expansion, we first get

$$\frac{\partial \mathbf{a}_a}{\partial t} + \mathbf{A} \nabla \mathbf{a}_a + (\operatorname{div} \mathbf{A}) \mathbf{a}_a = \mathbf{f} - \nabla p,$$

and then transforming the second left hand term according to a well known vector formula, we have

$$\frac{\partial a_a}{\partial t} + Aa_a\nabla + (\text{curl } a_a) \times A + (\text{div } A)a_a = f - \nabla p.$$

Now, the term $(\text{curl } a_a) \times A$ has appeared, which correspondingly appears in the expression $(IV., 8, E_1)$ for the force in the electric field, representing in one term the force exerted upon permanent polarization and upon magnetic current.

According to (a), the second term in the left hand member may be written

$$Aa_a\nabla = \alpha a_a a_a \nabla = \tfrac{1}{2}\alpha\nabla a_a^2,$$

or finally,

$$Aa_a\nabla = \nabla(\tfrac{1}{2}\alpha a_a^2) - \tfrac{1}{2}a_a^2\nabla\alpha.$$

Substituting this above, we have

$$\frac{\partial a_a}{\partial t} + \nabla(\tfrac{1}{2}\alpha a_a^2) - \tfrac{1}{2}a_a^2\nabla\alpha + (\text{curl } a_a) \times A + (\text{div } A)a_a = f - \nabla p,$$

giving us all the corresponding terms contained in the expression for the force $(IV., 8, E_1)$ in the electric field.

5. *Separation of the Equation of Motion.*—We thus seem to have found some relation between the hydrodynamic equation and the equation giving the dynamics of the electric field. But we still have the geometry and the dynamics of the hydrodynamic field united in one set of equations. To make the first step towards the separation of certain geometric and dynamic properties from one another we have to consider the hydrodynamic field as the sum of two partial fields, just as we consider the electric field as the sum of two partial fields, the induced and the energetic field. Let us represent the vector a_a, the actual specific momentum, as the sum of two vectors a and a_e, thus

$$(a) \qquad\qquad a_a = a + a_e.$$

The equation then develops into

$$(a') \quad \frac{\partial a}{\partial t} + \frac{\partial a_e}{\partial t} + \nabla(\tfrac{1}{2}\alpha a_a^2) - \tfrac{1}{2}a_a^2\nabla\alpha + (\text{curl } a_a) \times A$$
$$+ (\text{div } A)a_a = f - \nabla p.$$

Now we have the right to submit one of the auxiliary vectors, say **a**, to a condition. Let this condition be that it shall satisfy the equation

(b)
$$\frac{\partial \mathbf{a}}{\partial t} = -\nabla(p + \tfrac{1}{2}\alpha\mathbf{a}_a^2).$$

The other vector will then have to satisfy the equation

(c)
$$\frac{\partial \mathbf{a}_e}{\partial t} = \mathbf{f} - (\operatorname{div} \mathbf{A})\mathbf{a}_a + \tfrac{1}{2}\mathbf{a}_a^2\nabla\alpha - (\operatorname{curl} \mathbf{a}_a) \times \mathbf{A}.$$

6. *Geometric Property of the Induced Motion.* — We have thus introduced the consideration of two fields, which superimposed upon each other represent the actual hydrodynamic field. But the equations of both partial fields are still dynamic equations. However, from one of them we can at once proceed to a purely geometric equation. For taking the curl of equation (b) and changing the order of the operations $\partial/\partial t$ and curl, we get

$$\frac{\partial}{\partial t}\operatorname{curl} \mathbf{a} = 0.$$

To complete the nomenclature I will call the curl of the velocity the *kinematic*, and the curl of the specific momentum the *dynamic vortex density.* The dynamic vortex density is thus invariable at every point of space. Integrating with respect to the time and writing $-\mathbf{k}$ for the constant of integration, we get

(d)
$$\operatorname{curl} \mathbf{a} = -\mathbf{k},$$

which expresses the *local* conservation of the dynamic vortex density. As regards its form, this is the same equation which in the electric interpretation of the symbols expresses the relation between the electric field intensity **a** and the magnetic current **k** (IV., 8, *B*). And, as the conservation of **k** is local, equation (d) corresponds exactly to the equation for the electric field for the cases of magnetic currents which are stationary both in space and in time.

7. *Fundamental Geometric Properties of the Hydrodynamic Field.* —We have thus succeeded in representing the hydrodynamic field

as the sum of two partial fields. Writing $\mathbf{A}_e = \alpha \mathbf{a}_e$, we have for the vectors introduced the equation of connection

$$(A) \qquad \mathbf{A} = \alpha \mathbf{a}_a = \alpha \mathbf{a} + \mathbf{A}_e.$$

Then the induced field described by $\mathbf{a}$ has the property of local conservation of the dynamic vortex,

$$(B) \qquad \operatorname{curl} \mathbf{a} = -\mathbf{k},$$

while from the field of the actual velocity we calculate the velocity of expansion per unit volume, E, from the equation

$$(C) \qquad \operatorname{div} \mathbf{A} = E.$$

In form, these equations are precisely the fundamental equations for the geometric properties of the stationary electric field.

8. *Bodies and Fundamental Fluid.* — To complete the investigation of the geometric properties we shall have to examine whether we can introduce conditions corresponding to the supplementary conditions (IV., 8, D). The introduction of conditions of this nature for the fluid system evidently involves the distinction between certain limited parts of the fluid, which we have to compare with material bodies, and an exterior unlimited part of the fluid, which we have to compare with the free ether. The part of the fluid surrounding the *fluid bodies* we shall call the *fundamental fluid.*

Introducing the condition

$$(D_1) \qquad \alpha = \alpha_0,$$

where α_0 is constant, we simply require the fundamental fluid to be homogeneous. Introducing the condition

$$(D_2) \qquad E = 0,$$

we require it to be incompressible. There is nothing which prevents us from introducing the additional condition

$$(D_3) \qquad \mathbf{k} = 0,$$

for, at every point of space the dynamic vortex has, according to the fundamental equation (B), a constant value. We are therefore free to impose the condition that in the parts of space occupied by the fundamental fluid this constant shall have the value zero. This, in connection with the general condition (B), of course involves also a restriction upon the generality of the motion of the fluid bodies. The nature and consequence of this restriction will be discussed later, but for the present it is sufficient for us to know that nothing prevents us from introducing it.

The question now arises: are we also entitled to introduce for the hydrodynamic system a condition corresponding to the condition (D_3) for the ether? To answer this we must refer to the dynamic equation $(5, c)$. On account of the restriction (D_1), we shall have $\nabla a = 0$ in the fundamental fluid. On account of condition (D_2), we shall have div $\mathbf{A} = 0$, so that two of the right hand terms of the equation for the energetic motion disappear. Writing $a_a = a + a_c$ and remembering the condition (D_3), just introduced, we find curl $\mathbf{a}_a =$ curl $\mathbf{a}_e$, and the equation therefore reduces to

$$\frac{\partial \mathbf{a}_e}{\partial t} = \mathbf{f} - (\text{curl } \mathbf{a}_e) \times \mathbf{A}.$$

Furthermore, we are free to introduce the condition that the exterior force $\mathbf{f}$ shall be zero for every point in the fundamental fluid, so that the equation becomes

$$\frac{\partial \mathbf{a}_e}{\partial t} = - (\text{curl } \mathbf{a}_e) \times \mathbf{A}.$$

Now if at any point in space $a_e = 0$, we shall also have

$$\frac{\partial \mathbf{a}_e}{\partial t} = 0,$$

i. e., under the given conditions there can be no energetic field intensity a_e unless it existed previously. The same will be true of the energetic velocity $\mathbf{A}_e$, which is simply proportional to the corresponding field intensity a_e. Nothing prevents us, consequently, from requiring that in the space occupied by the fundamental fluid we shall have the condition

(D_4) $\mathbf{A}_e = 0$

always fulfilled. For evidently we have the right to introduce the condition (D_4) as an initial condition. And, as we have seen, if it is fulfilled once, it will always be fulfilled.

Summing up the contents of $(D_1) \cdots (D_4)$ we find that we have introduced the following conditions defining the difference between the fluid bodies and the surrounding fundamental fluid, which is analagous to the difference between the bodies and the surrounding ether in the electromagnetic field. The fundamental fluid has constant mobility (specific volume), just as the ether has constant inductivity; the fluid bodies may have a mobility varying from point to point and differing from that of the fundamental fluid; just as the bodies in the magnetic field may have an inductivity varying from point to point and differing from that of the ether. The fundamental fluid never has velocity of expansion or contraction, E, while this velocity may exist in the fluid bodies; just as in the free ether we have no distribution of true electrification or magnetism, while such distribution may exist in material bodies. The fundamental fluid never has a distribution of dynamic vortices, while such distributions may exist in the fluid bodies; just as the ether in the case of stationary fields never has a distribution of currents, electric or magnetic, while such distributions may exist in material bodies. The fundamental fluid never has an energetic velocity, while this velocity may exist in the fluid bodies; just as the ether never has an energetic (impressed) polarization, while such polarization may exist in material bodies.

Under these conditions the geometric properties of the hydrodynamic field and the stationary electric or magnetic field are described by equations of exactly the same form. Thus, under the given conditions, whose physical content we shall consider more closely later, there exists a perfect geometric analogy between the two kinds of fields.

9. *Dynamic Properties of the Hydrodynamic Field.* — It is easily seen that under certain conditions an inverse dynamic

13

analogy will be joined to this geometric analogy.   For let us impose the condition that

$$(a) \qquad \frac{\partial \mathbf{a}_e}{\partial t} = 0$$

shall always be satisfied, *i. e.*, that the energetic specific momentum shall be conserved *locally*.   When this condition is fulfilled, the equation of the energetic motion, which we will now have to use for the bodies only, reduces to

$$(b) \qquad \mathbf{f} = (\mathrm{div}\ \mathbf{A})\mathbf{a}_a - \tfrac{1}{2}\mathbf{a}_a^2 \nabla \alpha + (\mathrm{curl}\ \mathbf{a}_a) \times \mathbf{A},$$

i. e., if the condition of the local conservation of the energetic specific momentum must be fulfilled, there must act upon the system an exterior force **f**, whose distribution per unit volume is given by (*b*).   According to the principle of equal action and reaction, this force thus balances a force $\mathbf{f}_1$, exerted under the given conditions by the fluid system.   The fluid system therefore exerts the force

$$(E_1) \qquad \mathbf{f}_1 = - (\mathrm{div}\ \mathbf{A})\mathbf{a}_a + \tfrac{1}{2}\mathbf{a}_a^2 \nabla \alpha - (\mathrm{curl}\ \mathbf{a}_a) \times \mathbf{A},$$

which, in form, oppositely corresponds to the force which is exerted, according to HEAVISIDE's investigation, by the electric or the magnetic field in the corresponding case.

10. *Second Form of the Analogy.* — The physical feature of the analogy thus found is determined mainly by the condition (9, *a*) for the *local* conservation of the energetic specific momentum.   The physical content of this condition we will discuss later.   But first we will show that even other conditions may lead to an analogy, in which we do not arrive at HEAVISIDE's, but at some one of the other expressions for the distribution of force.

We start again with the equation of motion,

$$(a) \qquad \frac{1}{\alpha} \frac{d\mathbf{A}}{dt} = \mathbf{f} - \nabla p.$$

Now, instead of introducing the actual specific momentum $\mathbf{a}_a$, I introduce at once the induced specific momentum **a** and the energetic velocity **A**, according to the equation of connection

$$(b) \qquad \mathbf{A} = \alpha \mathbf{a} + \mathbf{A}_e.$$

Performing the differentiation and making use of the equation of continuity (2, *a*), we have

$$\frac{d\mathbf{a}}{dt} + (\operatorname{div} \mathbf{A})\mathbf{a} + \frac{1}{\alpha}\frac{d\mathbf{A}_e}{dt} = \mathbf{f} - \nabla p.$$

Introducing in the first left hand term the local time-derivation,

$$\frac{\partial \mathbf{a}}{\partial t} + \mathbf{A}\nabla\mathbf{a} + (\operatorname{div} \mathbf{A})\mathbf{a} + \frac{1}{\alpha}\frac{d\mathbf{A}_e}{dt} = \mathbf{f} - \nabla p,$$

or, transforming the second left hand member according to the vector formula,

(*c*) $$\frac{\partial \mathbf{a}}{\partial t} + \mathbf{A}\mathbf{a}\,\nabla + (\operatorname{curl} \mathbf{a}) \times \mathbf{A} + (\operatorname{div} \mathbf{A})\mathbf{a} + \frac{1}{\alpha}\frac{d\mathbf{A}_e}{dt} = \mathbf{f} - \nabla p.$$

Using the equation of connection (*b*) and performing simple transformations, we get for the second term in the left hand member

$$\mathbf{A}\mathbf{a}\nabla = \alpha\mathbf{a}\mathbf{a}\nabla + \mathbf{A}_e\mathbf{a}\nabla$$
$$= \tfrac{1}{2}\alpha\nabla\mathbf{a}^2 + \mathbf{A}_e\mathbf{a}\nabla$$
$$= \nabla(\tfrac{1}{2}\alpha\mathbf{a}^2 + \mathbf{A}_e\cdot\mathbf{a}) - \tfrac{1}{2}\mathbf{a}^2\nabla\alpha - \mathbf{a}\mathbf{A}_e\nabla.$$

Introducing this in (*c*),

(*d*) $$\frac{\partial \mathbf{a}}{\partial t} + \nabla(\tfrac{1}{2}\alpha\mathbf{a}^2 + \mathbf{A}_e\cdot\mathbf{a}) + \frac{1}{\alpha}\frac{d\mathbf{A}_e}{dt} + (\operatorname{div} \mathbf{A})\mathbf{a} - \tfrac{1}{2}\mathbf{a}^2\nabla\alpha$$
$$+ (\operatorname{curl} \mathbf{a}) \times \mathbf{A} - \mathbf{a}\mathbf{A}_e\nabla = \mathbf{f} - \nabla p.$$

Now, we can split the equation in two, requiring that the vector **a** satisfy the equation

(*e*) $$\frac{\partial \mathbf{a}}{\partial t} = -\nabla(p + \tfrac{1}{2}\alpha\mathbf{a}^2 + \mathbf{A}_e\cdot\mathbf{a}),$$

and we find that the other vector $\mathbf{A}_e$ must satisfy the equation

(*f*) $$\frac{1}{\alpha}\frac{d\mathbf{A}_e}{dt} = \mathbf{f} - (\operatorname{div} \mathbf{A})\mathbf{a} + \tfrac{1}{2}\mathbf{a}^2\nabla\alpha - (\operatorname{curl} \mathbf{a}) \times \mathbf{A} + \mathbf{a}\mathbf{A}_e\nabla.$$

Both equations are different from the corresponding equations (5, b) and (5, c). But, as is seen at once, the new equation for the induced motion involves the same geometric property as the previous one, namely, the local conservation of the dynamic vortex, expressed by (B). We arrive thus at the same set of fundamental geometric equations as before, (A) $\cdots$ (C). Furthermore, we have evidently the same right as before to introduce the restrictive conditions (D_1), (D_2), (D_3). A discussion of equation (f), similar to that given above for equation (5, d), shows us that we are entitled in this case also to impose the condition (D_4) upon the fundamental fluid, since in a fluid having the properties (D_1) $\cdots$ (D_3) a moving fluid particle cannot have an energetic velocity if this did not exist previously.

The geometric analogy therefore exists exactly as before, the conditions for its existence being changed only with respect to this one point, that the condition (D_4) now refers to the material particles belonging to the fundamental fluid, and not to the points in space occupied by this fluid. The consequence of this difference will be discussed later.

Finally, we see that to this geometric analogy we can add a dynamic analogy. Requiring that the energetic velocity be conserved *individually*, we have

(g) $$\frac{d\mathbf{A}_c}{dt} = 0,$$

and, reasoning as before, we find that under this condition the fluid system will exert per unit volume the force

(E_2) $\mathbf{f}_2 = -(\operatorname{div} \mathbf{A})\mathbf{a} + \tfrac{1}{2}\mathbf{a}^2 \nabla \alpha - (\operatorname{curl} \mathbf{a}) \times \mathbf{A} + \mathbf{a}\mathbf{A}_s \nabla,$

which, in form, oppositely corresponds to the forces in the electric or magnetic field, according to the expression (IV., 8 E_2).

11. We have thus arrived in two different ways at an analogy between the equations of hydrodynamic fields and those of the stationary electric or magnetic field. And, from an analytical point of view, this analogy seems as complete as possible, apart from the opposite sign of the forces exerted by the fields.

In regard to the closeness of this analytical anology, we have to remark that we do not know with perfect certainty which of the expressions (E_1) or (E_2), if either, represents the true distribution of the elementary forces in the electric or the magnetic field, while the corresponding distribution of forces in the hydrodynamic field are real distributions of forces which are exerted by the field and which have to be counteracted by exterior forces, if the conditions imposed upon the motion of the system are to be fulfilled. We cannot, therefore, decide which of the two forms that we have found for the analogy is the most fundamental. But we know with perfect certainty that, if we integrate this system of elementary forces for a whole body, we get the true value of the resultant force in the electric or magnetic field. When we limit ourself to the consideration of the resultant force only, the two forms of the analogy are therefore equivalent. And from the integration performed in the preceding lecture we conclude at once, that the resultant forces upon the bodies in the hydrodynamic field can also be represented as resulting from the fictitious distributions

(E_3) $\qquad \mathbf{f}_3 = - (\text{div } A)\mathbf{a} - A_j \mathbf{a} \bigtriangledown - (\text{curl } \mathbf{a}) \times A,$

and

(E_4) $\qquad \mathbf{f}_4 = - \alpha_0 (\text{div } \mathbf{a})\mathbf{a} - \alpha_0 (\text{curl } \mathbf{a}) \times \mathbf{a}.$

The fact, which we have just proved, that the laws of the electric or magnetic fields and of the hydrodynamic fields can be represented by the same set of formulæ, undoubtedly shows that there is a close relation between the laws of hydrodynamics and the laws of electricity and magnetism. But the formal analogy between the laws does not necessarily imply also a real analogy between the things to which they relate. Or, as MAXWELL expressed it: the analogy of the *relations* of things does not necessarily imply an analogy of the *things related*.

The subject of our next investigation will be, to consider to what extent we can pass from this formal analogy between the hydrodynamic formulæ and the electric or magnetic formulæ to an analogy of perfectly concrete nature, such as that represented by our experiments.

VI.

FURTHER DEVELOPMENTS AND DISCUSSIONS OF THE ANALOGY.

1. According to the systems of formulæ which we have developed, the hydrodynamic analogy seems to extend to the whole domain of stationary electric, or stationary magnetic fields. But according to our elementary and experimental investigation, we arrived at two different analogies which were wholly detached from each other. There is no contradiction involved in these results. In our analytical investigation we have hitherto taken only a formal point of view, investigating the analogy between the formal laws of hydrodynamics and of electromagnetism. If, from the analogy between the formal laws, we try to proceed further to an analogy between the different physical phenomena obeying them, we shall arrive at the two detached fragments of the analogy which we have studied experimentally.

2. Between the hydrodynamic and the electric or magnetic systems there is generally this important difference. The hydrodynamic system is moving, and therefore generally changing its configuration. But apparently, at least, the electric or magnetic systems with which we compare them are at rest. The correspondence developed between hydrodynamic and electromagnetic formulæ therefore gives only a momentary analogy between the two kinds of fields, which exist under different conditions.

To get an analogy, not only in formulæ but in experiments, we must therefore introduce the condition that the bodies in the hydrodynamic system should appear stationary in space. This can be done in two ways. First, the fluid system can be in a steady state of motion, so that the bodies are limited by surfaces of invariable shapes and position in space. Second, the fluid can be in a state of vibratory motion, so that the bodies perform small vibrations about invariable mean positions.

102

3. *Steady State of Motion.* — The first form of the analytical analogy, in which we supposed local conservation of the energetic specific momentum,

(a) $$\frac{\partial \mathbf{a}_r}{\partial t} = 0,$$

immediately leads us to the consideration of a perfectly steady state of motion, at which we arrive, if we assume besides (a) also the local conservation of the induced specific momentum,

(b) $$\frac{\partial \mathbf{a}}{\partial t} = 0,$$

which is perfectly consistent with (a).   But in the case of a steady state of motion the generality of the field is very limited, on account of the condition that the fluid, both outside and inside, moves tangentially to the stationary surface which limits the bodies.

4. *Irrotational Circulation Outside the Bodies.* — As the motion outside the bodies fulfills the condition curl $\mathbf{a} = 0$, and, in consequence of the constancy of the specific volume, α_0, also the condition curl $\mathbf{A} = 0$, the motion in the exterior space will be the well known motion of irrotational circulation, which is only possible if the space be multiply connected.   If, then, there is to be any motion of the exterior fluid at all, one or more of the bodies must be pierced by channels through which the fluid can circulate. Bodies which have no channels act only as obstructions in the current, which exists because of the channels through the other bodies.   The velocity or the specific momentum by which this motion is described has a non-uniform scalar potential.   The stream-lines are all closed and never penetrate into the interior of the bodies, but run tangentially to the surfaces.   The corresponding electrodynamic field, with closed lines of force running tangentially to the bodies and having a non-uniform potential, is also a well known field.

5. *Corresponding Field Inside the Bodies.* — This exterior field can correspond, in the hydrodynamic, as well as in the electro-

magnetic case, to different arrangements in the interior of the
bodies. The most striking restriction on the exterior field is the
condition that the lines of force or of flow shall never penetrate
into the bodies. In the magnetic case this condition will always
be fulfilled if the bodies consist of an infinitely diamagnetic
material, and a field with these properties will be set up by any
distribution of electric currents in these infinitely diamagnetic
bodies. The hydrodynamic condition corresponding to zero inductivity is zero mobility. The bodies then retain their forms
and their positions in space as a consequence of an infinite
density and the accompanying infinite inertia. Now in the case
of infinite density an infinitely small velocity will correspond to a
finite specific momentum. We can then have in these infinitely
heavy bodies any finite distribution of specific momentum and of
the dynamic vortex, which corresponds to the electric current, and
yet to this specific momentum there will correspond no visible
motion which can interfere with the condition of the immobility
of the bodies.

Other interior arrangements can also be conceived which produce the same exterior field. The condition of infinite diamagnetivity may be replaced by the condition that a special system
of electric currents be introduced to make bodies *appear* to be
infinitely diamagnetic. The corresponding hydrodynamic case will
exist if we abandon the infinite inertia as the cause of the immobility of the bodies and also dispense with the creation of any general distribution of dynamic vortices in the bodies, and if we introduce instead, special distributions of vortices, subject to the
condition that they be the vortices of a motion which does not
change the form of the bodies or their position in space. This
distribution of the dynamic vortices will, from a geometric point
of view, be exactly the same as the distribution of electric current
which makes bodies appear infinitely diamagnetic.

Finally, a third arrangement is possible. In bodies of any inductivity we can set up any distribution of electric currents, and
simultaneously introduce a special intrinsic magnetic polarization

which makes the bodies appear to be infinitely diamagnetic. Correspondingly, we can give to bodies of any mobility any distribution of dynamic vortices under the condition that we fix the bodies in space by a suitable distribution of energetic velocities produced by external forces.

6. *The Dynamic Analogy.* — In the cases thus indicated the geometric analogy between the fields will be perfect. And with this direct geometric analogy we have an inverse dynamic analogy. The system of elementary forces, by which the field tends to produce visible motions of the bodies, and which must be counteracted by exterior forces, oppositely corresponds in the two systems.

The simplest experiments demonstrating these theoretical results are those showing the attraction and the repulsion of rotating cylinders, and the attraction of a non-rotating, by a rotating cylinder, corresponding to the repulsion of a diamagnetic body by an electric current.

As the analogy thus developed holds for any arrangement of electric currents in infinitely diamagnetic bodies, it will also hold for the arrangement by which magnets can be represented according to AMPERE's theory. We can thus also get an analogy to magnetism, but in a peculiarly restricted way, since it refers only to permanent magnets constructed of an infinitely diamagnetic material. The hydrodynamic representation of a magnet is therefore a body pierced by a multitude of channels through which the exterior fluid circulates irrotationally. Such bodies will then exert apparent actions at a distance upon each other, corresponding inversely to those exerted by permanent magnets which have the peculiar property of being constructed of an infinitely diamagnetic material. This peculiar analogy was discovered by LORD KELVIN in 1870, but by a method which differs completely from that which we have followed here.

7. *Restricted Generality of the Field for the Case of Vibratory Motion.* — The hypothesis of a vibratory motion also restricts the generality of the field, but in another way than does the condition of steady motion. For, when the specific momentum is vibratory, its

14

curl, if it has any, must also be vibratory. But we have found that this curl, or the dynamic vortex density, is a constant at every point in space, and is thus independent of the time. The dynamic vortex therefore must be everywhere zero, and the equations expressing the geometric analogy reduce to

$$\mathbf{A} = \alpha\mathbf{a} + \mathbf{A}_e,$$

(a) $\operatorname{curl} \mathbf{a} = 0,$

$$\operatorname{div} \mathbf{A} = E,$$

with the conditions for the surrounding fluid,

(b) $\alpha = \alpha_0,$ $E = 0,$ $\mathbf{A}_e = 0.$

The equations thus take the form of the equations for the static electric, or the static magnetic field, so that the analogy will not extend beyond the limits of static fields. To establish the corresponding dynamic analogy we may use neither of the conditions (V., 9, a or 10, g). For both are contradictory to the condition for vibratory motion. We have to return to the unrestricted equation for the energetic motion, and the form which in this case leads to the most general results is (10, f), which according to (a) reduces to

(c) $$\frac{1}{\alpha}\frac{d\mathbf{A}_e}{dt} = \mathbf{f} - (\operatorname{div} \mathbf{A})\mathbf{a} + \tfrac{1}{2}\mathbf{a}^2\nabla\alpha + \mathbf{a}\mathbf{A}_e\nabla.$$

This system of equations is valid for any single moment during the vibratory motion. We shall have to try to deduce from it another system of equations which represents the invariable mean state of the system.

8. *Periodic Functions.* — To describe the vibratory motion we shall employ only one periodic function of the time, and therefore the different particles of the fluid will not have vibratory motions independent of each other. The motion of the fluid will have the character of a fundamental mode of an elastic system. To describe this fundamental mode we use a periodic function, f, of the period τ; thus

(a) $$f(t + \tau) = f(t).$$

The values of the function f should be contained between finite limits, but the period τ should be a small quantity of the first order. Further, the function f must be subject to the following conditions: during a period it shall have a linear mean value 0, and a quadratic mean value 1, thus

$$(b) \qquad \frac{1}{\tau}\int_t^{t+\tau} f(t)dt = 0,$$

$$(c) \qquad \frac{1}{\tau}\int_\tau^{t+\tau} [f(t)]^2 dt = 1.$$

Evidently these conditions do not restrict the nature of the function, provided it be periodic. Any periodic function may be made to fulfil them by the proper adjustment of an additive constant and of a constant factor. An instance of a function which fulfils the conditions is

$$(d) \qquad f(t) = \sqrt{2}\sin 2\pi\left(\frac{t}{\tau} + h\right).$$

From the conditions that the period is a small quantity of the first order and that the mean linear value of the function for a period is zero, it is deduced at once, that the time integral of the function over any interval of time multiplied by any finite factor n will never exceed a certain small quantity of the first order. We may thus write

$$(e) \qquad \int_t^{t''} nf(t)dt < \delta,$$

where n is a finite factor, and δ a certain small quantity of the first order.

9. *Representation of the Vibratory State of Motion by Quantities Independent of the Time.* — To get equations which define uniformly the vibratory motion we can now make use of the property of the field, that it is determined uniquely by the energetic velocity A in connection with the velocity of expansion E. The motion will thus be definitely determined by the two equations,

$$(a_1) \qquad A_s = A_{rm}f(t),$$

$$(a_2) \qquad E = E_m f(t),$$

where $\mathbf{A}_{em}$ and E_m are quantities independent of the time, but varying of course from particle to particle. As to their absolute values, these constants are the quadratic mean values of the energetic velocity $\mathbf{A}_e$ and of the velocity of expansion E. For, from equation (8, c), we get

$$\mathbf{A}_{em}^2 = \frac{1}{\tau} \int_t^{t+\tau} \mathbf{A}_e^2 dt,$$

$$E_m^2 = \frac{1}{\tau} \int_t^{t+\tau} E^2 dt.$$

The constants $\mathbf{A}_{em}$ and E_m for different particles in space may have different signs. These are always given by the equations (a_1) and (a_2), and the rule of signs may be expressed thus; the quantities $\mathbf{A}_{em}$ and E_m have respectively always the same sign as the variable quantities $\mathbf{A}$ and E had at a certain initial time. The absolute signs thus attributed to $\mathbf{A}_{em}$ and E_m have no great importance, but it is important that this rule determines perfectly the signs which the different quantities $\mathbf{A}_{em}$ and E_m have *relatively* to each other.

With regard to the motions determined by (a), we can conclude from the property (8, e) of the function f, that the energetic velocity produces displacements from the mean position of the particle, which never exceed a certain small quantity of the first order. And in the same way we conclude, that the change of volume produced by the periodic velocity of expansion and contraction never exceeds a small quantity of the same order. This has the important consequence that, neglecting small quantities of the first order, we can consider the specific volume, α, of the fluid as constant, except, of course, in cases where it has to undergo a differentiation with respect to the time.

According to this, it is easy to write the explicit expressions of the actual velocity $\mathbf{A}$ and of the specific momentum $\mathbf{a}$. Doing this,

(b_1) $$\mathbf{A} = \mathbf{A}_m f(t),$$

(b_2) $$\mathbf{a} = \mathbf{a}_m f(t).$$

For the substitution of these expressions and the expressions (a) in the equations $(7, a)$ shows that they satisfy them, if the quantities independent of the time satisfy the equations

(c)
$$\mathbf{A}_m = \alpha \mathbf{a}_m + \mathbf{A}_{cm},$$
$$\operatorname{curl} \mathbf{a}_m = 0,$$
$$\operatorname{div} \mathbf{A}_m = E_m,$$

in connection with the conditions for the exterior fluid

(d)
$$\alpha = \alpha_0, \qquad \mathbf{A}_{cm} = 0, \qquad E_m = 0.$$

If these equations be satisfied, (b) will satisfy the equations and represent *the* solution, as there exists but one.

The equations (c), which the quantities $\mathbf{A}_m$, $\mathbf{a}_m$, $\mathbf{A}_{cm}$, E_m, satisfy, have exactly the same form as the equations $(7, a)$. They give, therefore, for all times the same analogy to an invariable electromagnetic field as the corresponding variable quantities give for a single moment. The similarity is so great that it is not even necessary to introduce two sets of notation. To pass from the one form of the analogy to the other it is sufficient to change the signification of the letters in the equations $(7, a)$; if these quantities are interpreted, not as the velocities and the specific momenta themselves, but as representing in the indicated manner the mean intensities of these quantities, they give the geometric analogy existing at any time between the electric or magnetic field and the case of vibratory motion in the hydrodynamic field.

10. *The Mean Value of the Force in the Vibratory Field.*— Finally, to examine the dynamics of the field we have to substitute the expressions $(9, a)$ and $(9, b)$ in the equation of energetic motion $(7, c)$ and perform the integration over a period of the oscillations. Using the property $(8, b)$ of the function f, we find that the left hand member of the equation disappears. Designating by $\mathbf{f}'_m$ the mean value of the exterior force $\mathbf{f}$ and using the property $(8, c)$ of the function f, we find

$$0 = \mathbf{f}'_m - (\operatorname{div} \mathbf{A}_m)\mathbf{a}_m + \tfrac{1}{2}\mathbf{a}_m^2 \nabla \alpha + \mathbf{a}_m \mathbf{A}_{cm} \nabla.$$

This equation shows that during the vibratory state of motion the external force will have to balance a mean force exerted by the system, which has the value

$$\mathbf{f}_m = -(\operatorname{div} \mathbf{A}_m)\mathbf{a}_m + \tfrac{1}{2}a_m^2 \nabla\alpha + \mathbf{a}_m \mathbf{A}_{em}\nabla.$$

The expression has again exactly the same form as the expression for the force in the case of the momentary analogy, except that the varying quantities are replaced by quantities independent of the time. The similarity of the expressions makes it unnecessary to use two systems of notation. We can write the expression for the force

$$\mathbf{f}_2 = -(\operatorname{div} \mathbf{A})\mathbf{a} + \tfrac{1}{2}a^2 \nabla\alpha + \mathbf{a}\mathbf{A}_e \nabla,$$

and interpret, according to the circumstances, the quantities $\mathbf{a}$ and $\mathbf{A}$ as the momentary values of specific momentum and velocity, respectively or as the quantities which represent in the way indicated the mean intensities of these quantities. In one case we arrive at the analogy which exists for a moment only, in the other case at the analogy which exists independent of the time. Both analogies have the same degree of exactness, the geometric analogy being direct, and the dynamic analogy being inverse.

11. We have thus arrived at this result, that in the case of vibratory motion the hydrodynamic field can be described with reference to geometric properties by the following formulæ,

$$\mathbf{A} = \alpha\mathbf{a} + \mathbf{A}_e,$$

(a) $$\operatorname{curl} \mathbf{a} = 0,$$

$$\operatorname{div} \mathbf{A} = E,$$

together with the conditions for the fundamental fluid,

(b) $$\alpha = \alpha_0, \qquad E = 0, \qquad \mathbf{A}_e = 0.$$

And this fluid system, in the supposed vibratory state of motion, will exert exterior forces tending to produce visible motions, which are given by

(c) $$\mathbf{f}_2 = -(\operatorname{div} \mathbf{A})\mathbf{a} + \tfrac{1}{2}a^2 \nabla\alpha + \mathbf{a}\mathbf{A}_e \nabla.$$

In these equations all quantities are independent of the time.

But these equations are also the fundamental equations for an electrostatic or for a magnetic system, except for the difference that the force f_2 has the opposite direction. It is an open question whether this expression for the elementary forces in the case of the electric or magnetic field is fundamental, or only a fictitious force which gives the right value of the resultant force upon the whole body.

We have succeeded in proving this: the vibratory hydrodynamic field has the same geometric configuration as an electrostatic or a magnetic field. In the hydrodynamic field there are forces whose resultant upon finite bodies oppositely corresponds to the corresponding resultant forces in the electric or magnetic field.

To show that this result gives the full explanation of all our experiments with the pulsating and oscillating bodies we have only to add one remark. In our experiments we used pulsating and oscillating bodies constructed of solid material. On the other hand, in our mathematical developments we have considered the bodies as fluid. But these fluid bodies are subject to the action of forces which give the prescribed state of vibration, and which are subject to no restrictive conditions. Nothing prevents us, therefore, from adjusting these forces so as to give the fluid bodies the same motion as they would have if they were constructed of solid material. The reactions exerted upon them by the surrounding fluid will then of course be exactly the same as if they were constructed of solid material.

12. We have nothing to add to the demonstration of the analogy. But, to make ourselves better acquainted with it, we may make a simple application of it. In the analogy, for instance, pulsating particles produce fields of the same geometric configuration as electrically charged particles, and are acted upon by forces oppositely corresponding to those acting upon the latter. Pulsating particles will therefore act upon each other according to a law analogous to that of COULOMB, except for the reversed sign of the force. Introducing for the charges, or the intensities of pulsation of the two particles

$$\epsilon = \int E d\tau, \qquad \epsilon' = \int E' d\tau,$$

and using the rational system of units, we get for this law

$$F = -\frac{1}{\alpha_0} \frac{\epsilon \epsilon'}{4\pi r^2},$$

r being the distance between the two particles, and α_0 the inductivity, or the mobility of the medium.

Let us now imagine an investigator who observes the attraction and the repulsion of the pulsating bodies, but who is not capable of observing the water which transfers the action, or the pulsations which set up the field in the water. He will then believe that he sees an action at a distance, following a law having the same form as that governing the action at a distance between electrified particles.

Let us imagine that, as he proceeds in his further investigations, he moves one pulsating body, ϵ', from point to point in the space surrounding the other, measures at each point the force $\mathbf{F}$, and draws an arrow representing the value of $\mathbf{F}/\epsilon'$. He then arrives at the formal disposition of a field which is associated with the pulsating body ϵ. He has, no more than in the electrical case, a formal right to attribute to this field a physical significance, or to attribute to the recorded vector a physical existence. His experiments give him evidence only of this, that there is a force acting at the point where he places his second charge, ϵ'. But he has no evidence of the existence of a physical vector at this point after he has removed the charge ϵ'.

But in spite of this, he may try to change his view. He may imagine the existence of a medium which he does not see, and make the hypothesis that the vector represents some state existing, or some process going on, in this medium. In the electrical case we have no direct evidence that this hypothesis is correct, although thus far, the development of our knowledge of electricity makes it extremely probable that there must be some truth in it. But in the hydrodynamic case we have the full evidence: the medium exists; it is an incompressible fluid. And the vector recorded represents the specific momentum in the field set up in the fluid by the pulsating body. Thus we get a verification by analogy of the hypothesis which forms the basis of the whole modern theory of electricity.

13. But now let our hydrodynamic investigator proceed still further. Let him conclude with MAXWELL, that the attraction and repulsion between the pulsating bodies must depend upon a stress in the medium. Following MAXWELL's developments he will arrive at the expression of MAXWELL's stresses, with the reversed sign. But his conclusion in this case, that MAXWELL's stresses exist in the fluid and produce the attraction of the pulsating body, is wrong. The stress that exists in the fluid and produces the apparent actions at a distance is not MAXWELL's stress, but the isotropic stress or pressure in the fluid. We cannot conclude from this that MAXWELL's developments are also wrong for the electric field. But we have full evidence that they *may* be wrong, even in this case.

To return to the hydrodynamic case, it is easy to point out where the error comes in. MAXWELL *only* introduces his stresses to account for the forces which produce the visible motions. But in the hydrodynamic field the stress or pressure has a double task; first, to maintain the field, and second, to produce the visible motions. And it is extremely remarkable that the stress which has this double effect is a stress of much simpler nature than the stress imagined by MAXWELL, which produces only one of the two effects.

When we developed the electromagnetic equation of activity according to HEAVISIDE, we also met with the more general stresses introduced by him, which reduce in simple cases to MAXWELL's stresses. We cannot test HEAVISIDE's developments in the same way as MAXWELL's. For we have no hydrodynamic analogy extending to the electromagnetic phenomena of the most general type, from which he starts when he forms the equation of activity. But the fact remains that the

15

srtesses, even in HEAVISIDE's theory, are introduced only to explain
the visible motion observed in the field, not the formation or maintenance of the field itself   And even Heaviside gives, while emphasizing the importance of the stress-problem, in different forms
expression to the unsatisfactory nature of our present solution of
it   Thus

"Our attitude towards the general application of the special
form of the stress theory obtained should, therefore, be one of
scientific scepticism   This should, however, be carefully distinguished from an obstinate prejudice founded upon ignorance, such
as displayed by some anti-Maxwellians,   *

"It is natural to ask what part do the stresses play in the propagation of disturbances ?   The stresses and accompanying strains
in an elastic body are materially concerned in the transmission of
motion through them, and it might be thought that it might be
the same here   But it does not *appear* to be so from the electromagnetic equations and their dynamical consequences — that is to
say, we represent the propagation of disturbances by particular
relations between the space- and the time-variations of E and H,
and the electromagnetic stress and possible motions *seem* to be
accompaniments rather than the main theme "†

It may, therefore, be a question whether *this* will not be the
great problem in the theory of electricity, to find a stress which
accounts for both the formation and propagation of the electromagnetic field and for the visible motions of the charged or polarized bodies, just as the pressure in the fluid accounts for both the
formation of the hydrodynamic field and for the visible motions
of the pulsating or oscillating bodies

* Electromagnetic Theory, Vol 1, p 87
† *Loc. cit*, p 110

VII.

GENERAL CONCLUSIONS.

REMARKS ON METHODS OF RESEARCH AND OF INSTRUCTION IN THEORETICAL PHYSICS.

1. *The Problem of Fields of Force.*—We have in the preceding lectures taken the term " field of force " in a more general sense than usual. From the electric or magnetic fields we have extended this term also to the fields of motion in a perfect fluid. And this has been perfectly justified by the results obtained, the most striking of which is the extraordinary analogy in the properties of the two kinds of fields. So far as the analogy extends, there is one, and only one, difference, the reversed sign of the energetic forces. The relation of the electromagnetic and the hydrodynamic fields may be compared to the relation between an object and its image in a mirror ; every characteristic detail of the object is recognized in the image, but at the same time there is the characteristic difference that left and right are interchanged. But, however peculiar this difference may be, it cannot hide the common structure of the object and its image.

The discovery of this extraordinary analogy gives rise to several considerations, and one of the first is this : Has our research been exhaustive ? Are the phenomena investigated by us the only phenomena which have the same general structure as the electromagnetic phenomena, or can still other phenomena with corresponding fundamental properties be discovered ?

I think that it is very improbable that our investigation has been exhaustive. Even within the domain of hydrodynamics our investigation has probably been incomplete. There are, indeed, very strong indications that an analogy between electromagnetic and hydrodynamic fields may be found with quite another correspondence between the electric and the hydrodynamic quanti-

ties   And if we no longer limit ourselves to the consideration of
fluids, but pass to media of other and more general properties, we
may hope to find still other forms of the analogy, perhaps of even
greater generality

2 *Fields in Other Media than Fluids* — The question now
arises Are not the laws which we have found so entirely depen-
dent upon the fluid properties that it will be useless to look for
similar laws when we pass to other media? To answer this question we have to look for the origin of the hydrodynamic analogy
We then see that the geometric analogy had its origin to a great
extent in the equation of continuity   And, as this equation expresses the principle of the conservation of mass, it holds for any
material medium, and furnishes the same basis for a possible geometric analogy to electromagnetic fields

On the other hand, the dynamic properties of the hydrodynamic
fields had their origin principally in the inertia of the fluid masses
This is seen equally well in the elementary development of the
forces by the principle of kinetic buoyancy and in the mathematical
developments of Lecture V, where it is seen that the complete
expression of the energetic force develops from the inertia term of
the hydrodynamic equation of motion

A brief consideration thus shows that the principal conditions
from which the hydrodynamic analogy to the electromagnetic fields
developed, exist in any material medium, not alone in fluids
But the special form which the analogy will take, its accuracy, and
its extent, will depend upon the special properties of the different
media.   Thus the special properties of fluids admitted the existence of an analogy which is perfectly accurate, if we except the
inverse nature of the forces, but limited in extent   It will therefore be a most fascinating subject for research to examine whether
there exist media in which the accuracy of the analogy is pre-
served, while its scope is widened   Or, in other words, to determine the dynamic conditions of a medium in which the analogy,
with unaltered precision, has the greatest possible extent

3 *The Fields in a Transverse Elastic Medium* — To examine

the chances of progress along this line it will be advantageous to consider briefly the fields in a medium with the common elastic solid properties. Now it is well known that there is an extensive *geometric* analogy between the fields of motion in an elastic medium with properly adjusted constants and the electromagnetic fields of the most general type. The coexistence and equivalence of the two theories of light, the elastic and the electromagnetic, proves this perfectly. Indeed, the electromagnetic theory of light originated from the analogy which MAXWELL succeeded in stating between the equations for optical phenomena, developed by FRESNEL and his successors from the hypothesis of the transverse elastic ether, and the equations which he had himself developed to describe electromagnetic fields.

We will consider this analogy in the simplest possible case. Let the medium be homogeneous and isotropic, and, furthermore, incompressible and subject to the action of no exterior force. $\mathbf{U}$ being the vector displacement, α the specific volume, and μ the constant of transverse elasticity, the equation of motion of the medium is generally written

$$(a) \qquad \frac{1}{\alpha} \frac{\partial^2 \mathbf{U}}{\partial t^2} = \mu \nabla^2 \mathbf{U}.$$

As α and μ are constants, this may be written

$$\frac{\partial^2 \mathbf{U}}{\partial t^2} = \nabla^2 \alpha \mu \mathbf{U}.$$

On the right hand side of the equation we can now introduce the velocity

$$(b) \qquad \mathbf{A} = \frac{\partial \mathbf{U}}{\partial t}.$$

This member may at the same time be written in a modified form, the operation ∇^2 being, for the solenoidal vector $\mathbf{U}$, equivalent to $-\operatorname{curl}^2$. The equation may then be written

$$(c) \qquad \frac{\partial \mathbf{A}}{\partial t} = -\operatorname{curl}^2 \alpha \mu \mathbf{U} = -\operatorname{curl} \alpha^2 \mu \left(\operatorname{curl} \frac{1}{\alpha} \mathbf{U} \right).$$

Let us introduce now

(d) $$B = - \text{curl } \frac{1}{\alpha} U,$$

from which we get

$$\frac{\partial B}{\partial t} = - \text{curl } \frac{1}{\alpha} \frac{\partial U}{\partial t} = - \text{curl } \frac{1}{\alpha} A,$$

or, if we introduce the specific momentum a according to the equation

(e) $$A = \alpha a,$$

we have

(f) $$\frac{\partial B}{\partial t} = - \text{curl } a$$

On the other hand, the introduction of (d) in (c) gives

(g) $$\frac{\partial A}{\partial t} = \text{curl } \mu \alpha^2 B$$

If we introduce

$$b = \mu \alpha^2 B,$$

(g) finally takes the form

(h) $$\frac{\partial A}{\partial t} = \text{curl } b$$

Thus we can substitute for equation (a) the following system of equations

(i)

$$\frac{\partial A}{\partial t} = \text{curl } b,$$

$$\frac{\partial B}{\partial t} = - \text{curl } a,$$

where the vectors A and a, B and b are connected by the equations

(j)

$$A = \alpha a,$$

$$B = \beta b,$$

where β has the signification

(l) $$\beta = \frac{1}{\mu \alpha^2}$$

But this system is the system of MAXWELL's equations for a medium which is electrically and magnetically homogeneous and isotropic, and which is the seat of no intrinsic electromotive or magnetomotive forces.   And we get the following correspondence:

A   electric flux . . . . velocity
a   electric field intensity . . . specific momentum
B   magnetic flux . . . . curl of specific mass-displacement
b   magnetic field intensity . . (curl of sp. mass-displacement) μx^2
α   electric inductivity . . . . . . specific volume
β   magnetic inductivity . . . . density^2/coeff. of elasticity

As is well known, we are free to give different forms to this geometric analogy. We have used this freedom to choose a form which makes the analogy a direct continuation of the hydrodynamic analogy.

The extent of this geometric analogy is very great even though we have avoided full generality by neglecting heterogeneities and intrinsic forces. For it extends now to that point where the crossing of electric and magnetic phenomena takes place, the point at which the hydrodynamic analogy ceased.

4. *Dynamics of the Field in the Transverse Elastic Medium.* — These well known developments, which lead to the geometric analogy of electromagnetic and elastic fields, apparently give not the faintest indication of the existence also of a dynamic analogy, corresponding to that which we know from the investigation of the hydrodynamic field, which is quite the opposite of what we should expect from our preceding considerations.

The explanation of this apparent contradiction is, however, immediate. As we have remarked, the energetic force in the hydrodynamic fields originated in the inertia term of the hydrodynamic equation. But the equation of motion of the elastic medium, as it is generally written (3, *a*), contains this term incompletely, the local time derivation $\partial/\partial t$ being used as a first approximation for the individual derivation d/dt, which would give to the left member of the equation its proper form.

Let us repeat, therefore, the preceding development, but starting with the equation

$$(a) \qquad \frac{1}{\alpha}\frac{dA}{dt} = \mu\nabla^2 U + f,$$

in which the left member has its exact form, and in which we have added on the right hand side the exterior force f, which we suppose, however, small in comparison to the elastic forces. The left hand member of this equation is identical with the left hand member of the hydrodynamic equation, and may be developed in exactly the same way. We may thus write, as in (V, 10),

$$A = \alpha a + A_e,$$

and then equation (a) in the form

$$\frac{\partial a}{\partial t} + \nabla(\tfrac{1}{2}\alpha a^2 + A_e \cdot a) + \frac{1}{\alpha}\frac{dA_e}{dt} + (\operatorname{div} A)a - \tfrac{1}{2}a^2\nabla\alpha,$$
$$+ (\operatorname{curl} a) \times A - aA_e\nabla = \mu\nabla^2 U + f,$$

corresponding to (V, 10, d). As the medium is supposed homogenous and incompressible, this equation reduces to

$$\frac{\partial a}{\partial t} + \nabla(\tfrac{1}{2}\alpha a^2 + A_e \cdot a) + \frac{1}{\alpha}\frac{dA_e}{dt} + (\operatorname{curl} a) \times A$$
$$-aA_e\nabla = \mu\nabla^2 U + f$$

This may now be introduced in equation (a), and the equation then separated into two equations, just as in the case of the corresponding hydrodynamic equation. We thus arrive at the system of equations

$$(b) \qquad \frac{\partial a}{\partial t} = \mu\nabla^2 U - \nabla(aA_e + \tfrac{1}{2}\alpha a^2),$$

$$(c) \qquad \frac{1}{\alpha}\frac{dA_e}{dt} = f + aA_e\nabla - (\operatorname{curl} a) \times A,$$

where the first is that of the "induced," the second that of the "energetic" motion.

The first of these equations differs from equation (a) only by quantities of the order generally neglected in the theory of elasticity. If we agree to neglect these quantities, we may still describe the geometry of the field by the system of equations

$$\frac{\partial A}{\partial t} = \text{curl } b,$$

$$\frac{\partial B}{\partial t} = - \text{curl } a,$$

where now

$$A = \alpha a + A_e,$$

$$B = \beta b.$$

But if we proceed to the second approximation, we have, besides these equations describing the geometric configuration from time to time, to consider another partial motion, given by equation (e). And if we demand here that the energetic velocity be conserved individually, $dA_e/dt = 0$, we find that an exterior force f must be applied, which has the value

$$f = aA_e \bigtriangledown - (\text{curl } a) \times A.$$

This force inversely corresponds to the exterior force which had to be applied in the corresponding electromagnetic system, in order to prevent the production of visible motions due to the forces exerted by the system upon intrinsic electric polarization, corresponding to A_e, and upon magnetic current, — curl a.

5. This result thus gives a new and remarkable extension of the analogy. And the fact that continued research leads to further extension of the analogy between the formal laws of the phenomena, if not between the phenomena themselves, seems to indicate that there exists a common set of laws, *the laws of the fields of force*, where the expression fields of force is taken in a suitably extended sense. If this be true, the investigation of this common set of laws and the discovery of all phenomena obeying them will be one of the great problems of theoretical physics. And investi-

16

gations suggested by this idea may perhaps, sooner or later, lead
even to the discovery of the true nature of the electric or magnetic fields

6 But investigations of this kind can be considered as only
just begun   And if we return to our result relating to the
elastic field, it is easy to point out its incompleteness. In this
field we have not only the well known geometric analogy, but
also a dynamic analogy to the electrodynamic field, at least so
long as we confine our attention to the analogy between the
formal laws of the phenomena, and not to the phenomena themselves   And this dynamic analogy has exactly the same inverse
nature as in the case of the hydrodynamic field   But it should
be emphasized that this dynamic analogy, in the form in which
we have found it, has not the same degree of completeness as
the geometric analogy   I pass over here the fact that we have
given to our development only a restricted form, by supposing
the medium to be homogeneous and incompressible, and thus ex-
cluding beforehand heterogeneities and changes of volume   Most
likely this gap can be filled   But the great drawback is this   the
dynamics of the electromagnetic field relates to two classes of forces,
the electric forces and the magnetic forces, while our analysis of
the elastic field has led us to the discovery of only one class of
forces, namely, forces which correspond to the electric forces, according to our interpretation of them, but we have discovered
no trace of forces corresponding to the magnetic forces of the electromagnetic field   It is true that, making use of the symmetry,
we can change the interpretation, comparing from the beginning
the velocity with the magnetic, instead of the electric flux   The
elastic field will then, according to our analysis, give forces corresponding to the magnetic forces of the electromagnetic field, but
at the cost of the complete disappearance of the forces which previously corresponded to the electric forces

7 *Final Remarks on the Problem of Fields of Force.* — It is too
early of course to consider this incompleteness as a decisive failure
of the analogy in the elastic media   From the beginning there

seemed to exist no dynamic analogy at all. However, writing the inertia-term of the elastic equation in its correct form, we found at once forces corresponding to one class of forces in the electromagnetic field. But even in this form, the elastic equations will generally be only approximations. For the expression of the elastic forces is based upon HOOKE's law of the proportionality of the stresses to the deformations, and this law is an approximation only. Will the addition of the neglected terms, under certain conditions, bring full harmony between the electromagnetic and the elastic field? I put this question only to emphasize a problem which is certainly worth attention. If the research be carried out, it will certainly lead to valuable results, whether the answer turns out to be positive or negative. And even if the answer be negative, the investigation of the fields of force will not therefore be completed. It is not at all to be expected that the intrinsic dynamics of the electromagnetic field should correspond to that of one of the simple media of which we have a direct empirical knowledge. When the fields of these simple media are thoroughly explored, so that we know how far the analogy of their fields to those of electromagnetism goes, the time will then have come, I think, to put the problem in another form: What should be the properties of a medium, whose fields shall give the completest possible analogy to electromagnetic fields?

Even when the problem is put in this form, we have the advantage that preparatory work of great value has already been done. The gyrostatic ether, which was introduced by MacCULLAGH and LORD KELVIN, is a medium with very remarkable properties. As is well known, the fields in this medium give as perfect a geometric analogy to the electromagnetic field as the elastic medium. And the form of the expression for the energy in this medium seems to indicate the possibility of a dynamic analogy of greater extent than that which is likely to be found in the case of the common elastic medium.

It will be clear after these few remarks, that the problem of fields of force is of vast extent. We are only at the beginning of it.

8 *Kinetic Theories* — The problem of fields of force in this general sense evidently belongs to a class of problems which has been present in the minds of the natural philosophers from the very beginning of our speculations with regard to nature, but the method of stating the problem has changed

From the very first of human speculations on the phenomena of nature strong efforts have been made to construct dynamic models of these phenomena These dynamic models seem to be the natural way to render the phenomena of nature intelligible to the human mind I need only remind you of the efforts of the old philosophers of the atomistic school, such as DEMOK-RITOS or EPICURUS, or of philosophers of later time, like DES-CARTES Or I may mention a long series of theories of special physical phenomena, for instance HUYGHEN's, and NEWTON's theories of light, theories opposed to each other, but both of them dynamic theories Or I may remind you of the kinetic theory of gases of BERNOULLI, KRONIG, CLAUSIUS, and MAXWELL, or of MAXWELL's ingenious ideas of "physical lines of force"

But most of these speculations have broken down more or less completely Of the universal constructions of the atomists nothing is left except the building stones themselves, the atoms, which, however, have remained to this day an indispensable idea to the natural philosopher DESCARTES' theory of universal vortices had the same fate But though it fell, it left germs of fruitful ideas, leading in the direction of the fields of force NEWTON's theory of light also broke down But it did not exist in vain For the fact that phenomena of radiation could be explained according to his principle immensely facilitated the interpretation of the new phenomena of radiation, discovered in vacuum tubes and in radioactive substances The theory of light of HUYGHENS and FRESNEL is still unshaken, if it is considered merely as an abstract undulation theory But it is open to doubt whether it still exists in its original form as a theory which explains the phenomena of light on dynamic principles For a dynamic theory of light will hardly be satisfactory before we have a dynamic theory of electro-magnetism

This fate of dynamic theories which have had the unanimous support of all physicists may also bring into a dubious light dynamic theories which are still highly appreciated, as, for instance, the kinetic theory of gases. As a matter of fact, a strong reaction against dynamic theories has appeared.

9. *The Relation of Kinetic Theories to the Phenomenological Principles of Research.* — Reactions against exaggerations are always wholesome. On the other hand, it is a law of nature that reactions usually go to exaggerations. In accordance with this law, the energetic school developed. I will not enter upon the exaggerations of this school. But it has done good by emphasizing *phenomenological* research, the principles of which were developed especially by Professor MACH at Vienna, previous to the formation of the energetic school, and without its exaggerations.

The leading principle of Professor MACH is, that the phenomena of nature should be investigated with perfect impartiality and freedom from prejudice that the research should lead ultimately to a kinetic theory, or to any other preconceived view of natural phenomena. If this idea be carried out with perfect consistency, it is necessary, of course, not only that we should avoid the positive prejudice that the physical phenomena are ultimately phenomena of pure kinetics, but that we should also avoid the negative prejudice that the phenomena of nature are not ultimately kinetic. The principles of phenomenological research are therefore, rightly understood, not hostile to kinetic research, if this be only conducted with perfect impartiality.

If this be admitted, the extreme importance of kinetic research will not be denied by the adherents of the phenomenological principles of research. For no unprejudiced observer will deny that physical phenomena are inextricably interwoven with kinetic phenomena. Neither will he deny that our power of kinetic research exceeds by far our power of every other kind of physical research. The reason is obvious. We are all kinetic machines. Instinctive kinetic knowledge is laid down in our muscles and

nerves as an inheritance from the accumulated dynamic experience of our ancestors, and has been further developed without
interruption from the time of our first motions in the cradle   And
furthermore, while we have this invaluable instinctive knowledge
of the fundamental principles of dynamics, we have at the same
time an objective view of dynamic phenomena as of no other
physical phenomena, from the fact that we have the power of
following and controlling the phenomena of motion by several of
our senses at the same time, while for other phenomena, such as
sound, light, or heat, we have only one special sense, and for still
others such as electricity, magnetism, or radioactivity, we have
no special senses at all

No wonder, therefore, that at the time when science grew up
dynamics soon developed into the model science, from the formal
point of view the most perfect of physical sciences, and in this
respect second only to pure mathematics   This also explains why
the dynamic side of physical phenomena has always offered the
best point of attack for research, while, on the other hand, it gives
the obvious reason why we may be tempted to overestimate the
value of our dynamic constructions

But if a reaction against exaggeration has been necessary, nothing can be gained by giving up advantages which, for subjec-
tive reasons at least, are combined with the kinetic direction of
research, whatever be the final objective result of these researches
The reaction has taught us that problems should be stated in a
perfectly unprejudiced way

10   *The Comparative Method.* — It is such a way of conducting
the investigation of the relations between physics and kinetics,
which we have tried to realize in these researches on fields of force
The essence of the method is, that kinetic systems are made the
subject of pure phenomenological research   Their laws and properties are made the subject of impartial investigation, but with
constant attention to the analogies and the contrasts between the
laws found for the dynamic system and the laws of physical
phenomena

And this comparative method is applicable far outside the limits of our special problem of fields of force. Indeed, it is the method used by such authors as BOLTZMANN, HELMHOLTZ, HERTZ, and WILLARD GIBBS, in their profound researches in the dynamical illustration of physical laws and phenomena, especially those of heat and thermodynamics. These researches are uncompleted, just as are our researches on fields of force, and will probably remain so for a long time. But the more they have advanced, the stronger has been the demand for rigorousness of methods; the more have the methods of construction been forced back and the impartial comparative method advanced. And no one has emphasized conservative and safe methods more strongly than WILLARD GIBBS. In the preface to the last work which he has left us he expresses this in the following plain words:

"Difficulties of this kind have deterred the author from attempting to explain the mysteries of nature, and have forced him to be contented with the more modest aim of deducing some of the more obvious propositions relating to the statistical branch of mechanics. Here there can be no mistake in regard to the agreement of the hypotheses with the facts of nature, for nothing is assumed in that respect. The only error into which one can fall, is the want of agreement between the premises and the conclusions, and this, with care, one may hope, in the main, to avoid."

His method is exactly the same as that which we have tried to employ, namely the impartial research of each branch of physics by itself, but with comparison of the resulting laws, and with the greatest possible caution with respect to the conclusions to be drawn from the analogies and the contrasts presenting themselves. The method is that of comparative anatomy. Is it too sanguine a hope, that this method will, sooner or later, unveil for us the relations of the different physical phenomena, just as the methods of comparative anatomy successively give us an insight into the relation between the different kinds of living beings?

11. *On the Value of the Comparative Method for Instruction in Theoretical Physics.* — I cannot leave the discussion of this com-

parative method without seizing the occasion to emphasize its value also in instruction in theoretical physics. The results obtained by this method and the discovery of similar laws in apparently perfectly different branches of physics makes an unexpected concentration of instruction possible. And if the principle be carried out, and similar facts presented in similar ways, the analogies will facilitate, to a degree not to be overestimated, the power of the student to comprehend and assimilate the matter. Especially will this be the case when the analogies give us the opportunity to throw light upon obscure theories, such as those of the electromagnetic field, by means of perfectly plain and comprehensible theories such as those of the hydrodynamic field, in which every step can be made by rigorous mathematical conclusions, by elementary inductive reasoning, or by experiment.

And yet, this saving of labor, so imperatively demanded in our days whenever possible, is perhaps less essential in comparison with the independence relative to the methods and the results, which the student will gain when he observes how similar methods can be used, and similar laws obtained, in apparently widely different branches of physics. This will teach him to judge better the value of the methods, and give him independence of view for his future work as an investigator.

The arrangement of instruction according to principles by which the analogies at our disposal are used as much as possible for the benefit of the student, is a problem which has its own charm, involuntarily attracting the attention of the investigator engaged in research on these analogies. Time does not allow me to enter upon the details of my experiments in this direction. But before concluding these lectures, I wish to answer an objection, which seems to lie near at hand, against the use to a greater extent of these analogies in instruction.

12. *Theory and Practice.* — It seems to be an obvious reflection, that instruction conducted according to the plan thus indicated will be of an exceedingly abstract nature, tending to develop in a purely theoretical direction, and to draw attention away from

practically useful points. To take the nearest example: hydro-dynamics is useful if it teaches us to understand and calculate water motions occurring practically. Now water is practically homogeneous and incompressible, and hydrodynamics of practical use will have to direct the attention to the investigation of the motions of this simple medium, and not to the abstract fluid sys-tems considered by us, with density and compressibility varying according to laws never occurring practically.

I was of this opinion myself when I commenced my study of these extraordinary fluid systems. Nothing was further from my thoughts than to expect practical results from investigations of this abstract nature. But as the result of conversations with sci-entific friends who were interested in the dynamics of the ocean and the atmosphere, I happened to see that certain theorems which I had developed to investigate the motions of my abstract fluid system had immediate bearing upon the motion of these two media. And the reason why these theorems had not been discov-ered a long time before was obvious. To work out the science of the motion of fluids in a practical form investigators had always considered the fluids as homogeneous and incompressible, or, in the most general case, as compressible according to an idealized law, so that the density depended upon the pressure only. But these very suppositions precluded from consideration the primary causes of the motions in the atmosphere and the sea. For these primary causes are just the differences of density which do *not* depend upon the pressure, but on other causes, such as differences of temperature and salinity in the sea, and differ-ences of temperature and humidity in the atmosphere. While the old theorems of the practical hydrodynamics did not allow us to take up from the beginning the discussions of the circu-lations of the atmosphere and the sea, the thoerems which I had developed for my impractical fluid systems gave at once a very simple view of the atmospheric and oceanic circulations. If, there-fore, it be considered a question of practical importance to mas-ter the dynamics of these two universal media on which we

17

human beings are in such a state of dependence, then the methods of this theoretical hydrodynamics are not impractical. And I do not think that this is an isolated fact. For the more we advance in theoretical and practical research, the more we shall discover, I think, that there is really no opposition between theory and practice.

I hope that you will allow me to exemplify this in the additional lecture to-morrow, in which I shall consider the hydrodynamic fields of force in the atmosphere and the sea.

APPENDIX.

Vector Notation and Vector Formulæ.

A vector with the rectangular components A_x, A_y, A_z is designated by **A**.

A vector with the rectangular components B_x, B_y, B_z is designated by **B**.

A vector with the rectangular components C_x, C_y, C_z is designated by **C**.

Vector Sum. — The three scalar equations,

$$A_x + B_x = C_x,$$
$$A_y + B_y = C_y,$$
$$A_z + B_z = C_z,$$

are represented by one vector equation,

(1) $$\mathbf{A} + \mathbf{B} = \mathbf{C}.$$

C is called the vector sum of the two vectors **A** and **B**.

Scalar Product. — The scalar quantity $A_x B_x + A_y B_y + A_z B_z$ is designated by **A·B** and called the scalar or dot-product of the vectors **A** and **B**,

(2) $$\mathbf{A} \cdot \mathbf{B} = A_x B_x + A_y B_y + A_z B_z.$$

Vector Product. — The three scalar equations,

$$A_y B_z - A_z B_y = C_x,$$
$$A_z B_x - A_x B_z = C_y,$$
$$A_x B_y - A_y B_x = C_y,$$

are represented by one vector equation,

(3) $$\mathbf{A} \times \mathbf{B} = \mathbf{C}.$$

The vector **C** is called the vector- or cross-product of the two vectors **A** and **B**. The definition states that the vector product

131

C is normal to each of the vector-factors **A** and **B**, and is directed so that the positive rotation according to the positive screw rule around the vector **C** rotates the first vector-factor, **A**, towards the second, **B**. Change of the order of the factors, therefore, changes the sign of the vector-product.

Triple Products. — In a scalar product one vector-factor can be a vector-product. For this triple product it is easily proved that dot and cross can be interchanged, and that circular permutation of the factors is allowable, thus

(4)
$$\mathbf{A} \cdot \mathbf{B} \times \mathbf{C} = \mathbf{C} \cdot \mathbf{A} \times \mathbf{B} = \mathbf{B} \cdot \mathbf{C} \times \mathbf{A}$$
$$= \mathbf{A} \times \mathbf{B} \cdot \mathbf{C} = \mathbf{C} \times \mathbf{A} \cdot \mathbf{B} = \mathbf{B} \times \mathbf{C} \cdot \mathbf{A}.$$

In a vector-product one factor itself may be a vector-product. Cartesian development easily gives the formula

(5)
$$\mathbf{A} \times (\mathbf{B} \times \mathbf{C}) = -(\mathbf{A} \cdot \mathbf{B})\mathbf{C} + (\mathbf{A} \cdot \mathbf{C})\mathbf{B}.$$

Linear Derivation of a Scalar Quantity. — The three scalar equations,

$$A_x = \frac{\partial \alpha}{\partial x},$$

$$A_y = \frac{\partial \alpha}{\partial y},$$

$$A_z = \frac{\partial \alpha}{\partial z},$$

are represented by one vector equation,

(6)
$$\mathbf{A} = \nabla \alpha.$$

The differentiating symbol ∇ or "del" represents a vector operation with the three component-operations $\partial/\partial x$, $\partial/\partial y$, $\partial/\partial z$. The vector **A** or $\nabla \alpha$ shows the direction of greatest increase of the values of the scalar function α, and represents numerically the rate of this increase. The vector $-\nabla \alpha$ is called the gradient of the scalar quantity α (compare the classical expressions pressure-gradient, temperature gradient, etc.).

Spherical Derivation of a Scalar Quantity. — The sum of the second derivations of a scalar quantity may be called the spherical derivative of this quantity, and the operation of spherical derivation may be designated by ∇^2, thus

$$(7) \qquad \frac{\partial^2 \alpha}{\partial x^2} + \frac{\partial^2 \alpha}{\partial y^2} + \frac{\partial^2 \alpha}{\partial z^2} = \nabla^2 \alpha.$$

Divergence. — The scalar quantity $\partial A_x/\partial x + \partial A_y/\partial y + \partial A_z/\partial z$ is called the divergence of the vector **A**, and designated by div **A**, thus

$$(8) \qquad \frac{\partial A_x}{\partial x} + \frac{\partial A_y}{\partial y} + \frac{\partial A_z}{\partial z} = \text{div } \mathbf{A}.$$

Curl. — The three scalar equations,

$$\frac{\partial A_z}{\partial y} - \frac{\partial A_y}{\partial z} = C_x,$$

$$\frac{\partial A_x}{\partial z} - \frac{\partial A_z}{\partial x} = C_y,$$

$$\frac{\partial A_y}{\partial x} - \frac{\partial A_x}{\partial y} = C_z,$$

define a vector C, which is called the curl of the vector **A**, and the three scalar equations are represented by the one vector equation,

$$(9) \qquad \text{curl } \mathbf{A} = \mathbf{C}.$$

Spherical Derivation of a Vector. — The three scalar equations,

$$\frac{\partial^2 A_x}{\partial x^2} + \frac{\partial^2 A_x}{\partial y^2} + \frac{\partial^2 A_x}{\partial z^2} = C_x,$$

$$\frac{\partial^2 A_y}{\partial x^2} + \frac{\partial^2 A_y}{\partial y^2} + \frac{\partial^2 A_y}{\partial z^2} = C_y,$$

$$\frac{\partial^2 A_z}{\partial x^2} + \frac{\partial^2 A_z}{\partial y^2} + \frac{\partial^2 A_z}{\partial z^2} = C_z,$$

define the vector **C**, which is called the spherical derivative of **A**, and the three scalar equations are represented by one vector equation,

(10) $$\nabla^2 \mathbf{A} = \mathbf{C}.$$

Linear Operations. — The three equations,

$$A_x \frac{\partial B_x}{\partial x} + A_y \frac{\partial B_x}{\partial y} + A_z \frac{\partial B_x}{\partial z} = C_x,$$

$$A_x \frac{\partial B_y}{\partial x} + A_y \frac{\partial B_y}{\partial y} + A_z \frac{\partial B_y}{\partial z} = C_y,$$

$$A_x \frac{\partial B_z}{\partial x} + A_y \frac{\partial B_z}{\partial y} + A_z \frac{\partial B_z}{\partial z} = C_z,$$

may be represented by one vector equation,

(11) $$\mathbf{A}\nabla\mathbf{B} = \mathbf{C}.$$

The three scalar equations,

$$A_x \frac{\partial B_x}{\partial x} + A_y \frac{\partial B_y}{\partial x} + A_z \frac{\partial B_z}{\partial x} = C_x',$$

$$A_x \frac{\partial B_x}{\partial y} + A_y \frac{\partial B_y}{\partial y} + A_z \frac{\partial B_z}{\partial y} = C_y',$$

$$A_x \frac{\partial B_x}{\partial z} + A_y \frac{\partial B_y}{\partial z} + A_z \frac{\partial B_z}{\partial z} = C_z',$$

may be represented by one vector equation,

(12) $$\mathbf{AB}\,\nabla = \mathbf{C}'.$$

Between the two vectors defined by (11) and (12) there is the relation

(13) $$\mathbf{A}\,\nabla\,\mathbf{B} = \mathbf{AB}\,\nabla + (\text{curl } \mathbf{B}) \times \mathbf{A}.$$

Special Formulæ of Transformation. — The following formulæ are easily verified by cartesian expansion :

(14) $$\text{div } \alpha\mathbf{A} = \alpha \text{ div } \mathbf{A} + \mathbf{A} \cdot \nabla\, \alpha,$$

$$(15) \qquad \text{div} (\mathbf{A} \times \mathbf{B}) = -\mathbf{A} \cdot \text{curl } \mathbf{B} + \mathbf{B} \cdot \text{curl } \mathbf{A},$$

$$(16) \qquad \text{curl} (\alpha \triangledown \beta) = \triangledown \alpha \times \triangledown \beta.$$

If the operation curl be used twice in succession, we get

$$(17) \qquad \text{curl}^2 \mathbf{A} = \triangledown \text{ div } \mathbf{A} - \triangledown^2 \mathbf{A}.$$

Integral Formulæ. — If $d\mathbf{r}$ be the element of a closed curve and $d\mathbf{s}$ the element of a surface bordered by this curve, we have

$$(18) \qquad \int \mathbf{A} \cdot d\mathbf{r} = \int \text{curl } \mathbf{A} \cdot d\mathbf{s}$$

(Theorem of Stokes). If $d\mathbf{s}$ be the element of a closed surface, whose normal is directed positively outwards, and $d\tau$ an element of the volume limited by it, we have

$$(19) \qquad \int \mathbf{A} \cdot d\mathbf{s} = \int \text{div } \mathbf{A} d\tau.$$

Transformation of Integrals Involving Products. — Integrating the formula (16) over a surface and using (18), we get

$$(20) \qquad \int \alpha \triangledown \beta \cdot d\mathbf{r} = \int \triangledown \alpha \times \triangledown \beta \cdot d\mathbf{s}.$$

Integrating (14) and (15) throughout a volume and using (19), we get

$$(21) \qquad \int \mathbf{A} \cdot \triangledown \alpha d\tau = -\int \alpha \text{ div } \mathbf{A} d\tau + \int \alpha \mathbf{A} \cdot d\mathbf{s},$$

$$(22) \qquad \int \mathbf{A} \cdot \text{curl } \mathbf{B} d\tau = \int \mathbf{B} \cdot \text{curl } \mathbf{A} d\tau - \int \mathbf{A} \times \mathbf{B} \cdot d\mathbf{s}.$$

If in the first of these integrals either α or $\mathbf{A}$, in the second either $\mathbf{A}$ or $\mathbf{B}$, is zero at the limiting surface, the surface integrals will disappear. When the volume integrals are extended over the whole space, it is always supposed that the vectors converge towards zero at infinity at a rate rapidly enough to make the integral over the surface at infinity disappear.

Performing an integration by parts within a certain volume of each cartesian component of the expressions (11) and (12) and supposing that one of the vectors, and therefore also the surface-integral containing it, disappears at the bounding surface of the volume, we find, in vector notation,

$$(23) \qquad \int \mathbf{A} \bigtriangledown \mathbf{B} d\tau = - \int \mathbf{B} \ \mathrm{div} \ \mathbf{A} d\tau,$$

$$(24) \qquad \int \mathbf{AB} \bigtriangledown d\tau = - \int \mathbf{BA} \bigtriangledown d\tau.$$

Integrating equation (13) and making use of (23), we get

$$(25) \qquad \int \mathbf{B} \ \mathrm{div} \ \mathbf{A} \ d\tau = - \int \mathbf{AB} \bigtriangledown d - \tau \int (\mathrm{curl} \ \mathbf{B}) \times \mathbf{A} \ d\tau.$$

For further details concerning vector analysis, see: Gibbs-Wilson, Vector Analysis, New York, 1902, and Oliver Heaviside, Electromagnetic Theory, London, 1893.

CPSIA information can be obtained at www.ICGtesting.com
Printed in the USA
LVOW022203171212

312070LV00014B/787/P

9 781177 486323